Lily —
Thanks for your support. I hope
you find my Jungian journey
helpful in finding self-discovery.
~ Paul

Think Jung!

How I Found Meaning
in My Life

Cover Design by Andrew Wortman
Background courtesy of NASA, ESA, and the Hubble Heritage Team

ISBN: 1449996604
EAN-13: 9781449996604
LCCN: 2011901132

Think Jung!

How I Found Meaning in My Life

A Memoir

Paul Marshall Wortman

For Camille, Jer, Andrew, and Katie—
My Special Quaternity

Table of Contents

List of Dreams x

List of Photographs x

List of Poems x

Foreword: A Letter from Elaine N. Aron xiii

Preface: Letter for the Times xvii

Acknowledgments xix

Introduction xxi

Prologue: Why I Retired xxv

I Childhood Influences I
   I Remember Fanny I
   D-Day 6
   You're an INFP 9
   My Sinful Youth, or the Margaret Kennedy Affair 14
   Water Torture 17

2 Marriage 21
   I Was Married by the ACLU 21
   The Seven-Year Itch 25
   Christmas Tree Complexes 29
   My Fortieth Anniversary 32

3 Career **35**

    Miss MM 35

    St. Don and the Beard 39

    My Work: School Desegregation Research 43

    My Work: The Consensus Development

    Program Evaluation 47

    The New Year: Farewell to the First Half of Life 52

4 Loss **55**

    My Year of Death: Mother 55

    My Year of Death: Alan 61

    My Year of Death: Meghan 68

    Max 73

5 Complexes **79**

    Facing the Father-Complex 79

    Sh*t Happens 85

    "Remember to Fight the Dragon" 91

    An Encounter with the Mother-Complex 94

6 Family **99**

    Andrew's Secrets 99

    Quaternity 103

    My Son's Big, Fun Wedding 107

    The Turning Point: Quaternity Redux 116

7 Culture and Politics **123**

    Southern Hospitality 123

    Willy, Jim, and Dave 128

    September 11, 2006 133

    Another Letter for the *Times* 139

    The Parthenon Marbles 142

8 Anima Issues **149**

    Karin 149

    Valentine's Day 2008 160

    The Death of My Father-Complex 161

9 Health **167**

    My House was not My Home 167

    Black Day, White Knight 171

    Synchronicity 178

    My Right Foot. 182

10 Spirituality. **187**

    Alchemy 187

    Project Apollo 190

    The Return: My Transcendent Function 195

    In the Valley of the Gods: A Prayer on the Path 199

Afterword: Who Am I?. **201**

References 205

About the Author 209

List of Dreams

Healing Dream xxx
Facing the Father complex 79
Steam/Scream Dream 96
Journey Dream 119
Nobel Prize 196

List of Photographs

Fanny and Robert Mushnitsky 5
The author and his wife, Camille, at Pegasus 34
Donald T. Campbell 39
The author at Northwestern University, 1974 40
Graduation, 1999: The author with Carmelina Lalley 53
Andrew Wortman with his research poster 106
Katherine Waite and Jeremy Wortman 112
Celebrating the Obama Victory 127
The author with his flag quilt and 9/11 poem 138
The author at the Parthenon 143
Earth from space: "The Blue Marble" 197
The Valley of the Gods, Utah 200

List of Poems

The Potato Chip Man 8
Connecticut Derby, or How I Found My Brain 10
Emptying My Office and Finding What I Lost 52
Mother: In Memoriam 59
To Alan A Farewell Remembrance 64
The Paper Bag 66
At the Monastery 71
Dad: In Memoriam 76
Facing My Father 83
Recovered Memory 88
Embracing Job 89

Questions for My Father 92

Security. 101

Linger 105

Quintet 113

September 11, 2001 135

In Memoriam Day. 137

Healing Athena. 144

At the British Museum 146

Our Odyssey 151

Valentine's Day 160

We Are One. 193

In the Valley of the Gods: A Prayer on the Path. 199

Jung's Dharma. 204

The Word to Cherish. 210

Meaning makes a great many things endurable—perhaps everything.

—Carl Gustav Jung

Foreword:
A Letter from Elaine N. Aron

Tiburon, CA
June 14, 2010

Dear Paul,

I'm glad you are having a special birthday and are celebrating your seven decades by completing your memoirs. It gives me the delightful opportunity to reflect on you.

First, I feel a special bond with you because we are both HSPs (Highly Sensitive Persons) who have struggled with early childhood issues that have led to all sorts of fears and complexes. At the same time, I like our differences too, especially watching sensitivity in its masculine form, firsthand.

What stands out to me, however, are the changes in you that I've seen since I've known you that are reflected in your memoirs. You retired. A brilliant move. You chose soul over income. You recognized that after all of those academic pursuits, and in spite of your high intelligence and competence in methodology, you were really a feeling type in a resolutely thinking environment.

As a result of embracing that, the poet and Jungian in you blossomed, giving you life, the life of those around you, and your memoirs, too, a depth that keeps growing with time. What a smart move. Then you worked on yourself, and everyone around you can feel those changes. Not many people can say they have changed so much in later life. You used your brain to free your heart. Hurray for you!

Another one of your greater strengths is your willingness to face your shadow and work with it, to move into the symbolic realm rather than acting out, which requires great self-restraint, I know. And you have done this on your own, without an analyst. Even Jung couldn't do that.

As you get older, I appreciate more how much you retain a youthful spirit and *joie de vivre*. It makes you fun to be with. Meanwhile, as you deal with the body's aging, you seem to me to be enormously patient, Buddha-like, or at least you are low on that human compulsion to talk about these things in a way that dominates conversation and stands in the way of being in the moment.

Of course I very much admire how you are with Camille. If you are angry about the mistakes, you do not bear a grudge or use it against her. Rather, you go on supporting her, standing up for her and beside her. (And you do the same for Andrew.) It's difficult to keep marriage vows for decades as others slide away or minimize their importance. You have not only done that, but also increased the depth of your marriage as the years have passed.

I also love how you are there for others besides Camille. You have an enormously generous heart. Your psyche with its natural healing impetus got together with your loved ones, as we know the psyche does (being *social* psyche-ologists), to create deep change. How slow these changes are, but it does seem as though you work and work, and then something finally tips the scales, and it is more or less solid after that. Further, others around you benefit from the healed you, love even more this new you, and that really makes it solid.

Congratulations on a memoir-able birthday.

Love,

Elaine

Elaine N. Aron, PhD is a Jungian-trained analyst and author of *The Highly Sensitive Person* (1996) and, most recently, *the undervalued self* (2010)

Preface:
Letter for the *Times*

...we cannot live the afternoon of life according to the programme of life's morning; for what was great in the morning will be little at evening, and what in the morning was true will at evening be a lie.

—C.G. Jung (1969c, 399)

In a June 21, 2005, *New York Times* op-ed column, John Tierney proposed "the Adams Principle," whereby retirees follow the example of our sixth president, John Quincy Adams, by continuing to work in a "lesser job." I have followed the advice so eloquently stated above by Carl Jung and used this time in the second half of life to pursue my own growth, or "individuation" as Jung called it. I wrote the following letter expressing this view.

To the Editor:

From a psychological perspective, John Tierney has gotten both the "work ethic" and the president wrong. The latter stage of life should not replicate what we have done before, but should prepare us for the diminution of our powers through a focus on compassion, wisdom and good social works.

The model for this is former President Jimmy Carter. The Carter Principle includes a quiet spirituality that leads by compassionate example rather than political bullying, creative works such as books, including poetry, that add to our culture and self-knowledge, and good social works such as building homes for the homeless, supervising democratic elections and undertaking special missions of peace.

This is the important work ethic that retirees should engage in rather than be urged to continue to work in unfulfilling and unenlightening jobs that neither enrich them nor their fellow human beings.

Published by *The New York Times* on June 25, 2005.

Acknowledgments

As far as we can discern, the sole purpose of human existence is to kindle a light in the darkness of mere being.

—C. G. Jung (1989, 326)

This book is the result of work done in the Memoir Writing workshop of the Osher Lifelong Learning Institute (OLLI) at Stony Brook University. I thank the workshop leaders, Sheila Bieber and Dorothy Schiff Shannon, for creating an incredibly secure and supportive environment where such sensitive memoirs can blossom and one's writing can flourish. I also must thank two of my memoir-writing classmates, Jim Roth and Maria Tonkiss, for both their encouragement and example that it is possible to publish one's memoirs. In particular, I owe a special debt to my memoir-writing colleague and friend, Grace Papagno, who has consistently provided detailed comments and generous support for my writing. And, to all the workshop members who over the years have made constructive comments, I offer a heartfelt "thank you" for the many improvements reflected in the following pages.

This book presents an odyssey of growth and fulfillment inspired by and accomplished with my own personal Penelope, my wife, Camille. For every beautiful mountain we have climbed together there has been a dark valley that we have given each other the strength to cross. My children, Jeremy and Andrew, have also been part of the journey. Their love and support have taught me the true meaning of fatherhood.

Finally, this book represents a personal tribute to the insightful genius of the depth psychologist, Carl Gustav Jung. His concepts have unlocked the doors to numerous mysteries in my life. I have tried in these memoirs to illustrate just how Jung's many contributions have allowed me to unravel complex events. Jung has provided the necessary tools to put the jigsaw pieces of my life together into a meaningful whole. My hope is that you, too, will be able to use them as well. For all of this I am immensely indebted to my good friend, author, and Jungian psychotherapist, Elaine N. Aron, who encouraged me to *Think Jung!*

Introduction

And I have dream'd that the purpose and essence of the known life, the transient, Is to form and decide identity for the unknown life, the permanent.

—Walt Whitman, To Think of Time

In 1997, a colleague of mine, Professor Paul Dolan of the English Department, asked if I'd be willing to teach an upper-level undergraduate course called Psychology and Literature. The dean of the college had set up this special course and had asked him to teach it. He was too busy, but said he knew someone who could handle it—me. I readily agreed, and it was here that my experience with the Swiss depth psychologist Carl Gustav Jung began.

In casting about for a framework to tie all the readings together, my friend, Elaine Aron, suggested a Jungian perspective using James Hillman's (1977) book, *Re-visioning Psychology*. Although the course went remarkably well, it was not a smooth introduction to Jung as Hillman was not easily penetrated and didn't always agree with Jung. And I had never studied Jung before. Nonetheless, my interest had been aroused and soon I was immersed, feeling my way through Jung's concepts of anima/animus, archetype, collective unconscious, complex, individuation, self, and synchronicity, among others, through a variety of workshops and courses.

Despite the high ratings for my new Jung-oriented course, my departmental chair refused to allow me to teach it unless I could persuade the dean to continue paying for it. Consequently, I had to wait a few years until I retired, at which time I decided to offer an introductory workshop on Jung to the retirement learning group I joined. In the meantime, I'd found a wonderful book that introduces Jungian concepts to a lay audience—*Jung to Live By* written by Eugene Pascal (1992). Over the past five years, I have offered that course a number of times as well as others on Jungian dream analysis and Jungian interpretation of myths and fairy tales.

Unlike Freud, who claimed the unconscious was a repository of repressed sexual desires, Jung viewed it as a way to restore the imbalance caused by the problems encountered in conscious life. Dreams for Jung are messages from the unconscious that provide a major source of material to achieve such balance, typically through a minor adjustment or "compensation" in one's attitudes and behavior. They often reveal unconscious blocks or complexes, such as the well-known Oedipus complex first articulated by Freud, which are the cause of neurotic behavior. Jung extended this to a range of issues other than the sexual that he called the "father-complex." According to Jung, we all have father, mother, money, and a variety of other complexes which if severe (or negative) enough can result in significant life problems that prevent growth or, as he called it, "individuation."

The memoirs in this book illustrate how the various Jungian concepts can explain and help resolve important problems I encountered. Five dreams are presented and interpreted, including two in great detail (see Facing the Father-Complex in chapter 5 and Journey Dream, in The Turning Point: Quaternity Redux in chapter 6) with the latter one presented as a didactic exercise to help the reader with his or her own dreams. All dreams, according to Jung, contain a message or moral imperative that, if heeded, leads to healing, greater growth or individuation, and better balance in one's psychic life.

Jung also used a variety of creative tools such as sand play, or sand tray, and painting to get his patients to express their unconscious thoughts and feelings. The creative expression that has worked for me has been poetry. Twenty-five poems are included that illustrate my thoughts and feelings.

The ultimate goal of this journey is to encounter the most important archetype in the Jungian pantheon, the "self," which contains, according to Jung, the *imago Dei* or the image of God. Jung came from a long line of pastors and, unlike most psychologists, he was a fervent believer in God, if not the formalities and dogma that characterize current religions that he thought kept one from having a truly religious or numinous experience. I have been fortunate to have such a spiritual encounter (see My Nobel Prize Dream in chapter 10 of this book). For this I am thankful for Jung's concepts and dream analyses that have led me to a more fulfilling and meaningful life. My hope is that they will provide similar guidance and inspiration to you.

Prologue: Why I Retired

*a mighty hand guides us without fail to our destiny, and
not always is this hand a kindly one.*

—C. G. Jung (1985, 239)

I retired in the fall, 2001 after 34 years of university teaching of
which the last 12 years were at Stony Brook University (SBU).
Prior to that I'd had a very successful academic career. After a
shaky start at Duke (see the Miss MM section in chapter 3), I
rose from being a research associate to a tenured associate
professor of psychology at Northwestern University (see the
St. Don and the Beard section of chapter 3). From there I joined
the faculty at the University of Michigan in Ann Arbor, where
I was promoted to full professor in both public health and psychology. During that time, I served on many federal grant review committees, received a major award for my research, and
was elected president of the main professional organization in
my field (see the My Work sections in chapter 3). After all these
accomplishments, I would love to say that I retired at age sixty-
one with a feeling of satisfaction and the appreciation of my colleagues. Such was not the case. Fate came knocking at my door,
and when, at first, I refused to listen, it kept on knocking and
knocking until I, like Oedipus, got the message.

A few years after joining the faculty of the SBU Psychology Department, the chairperson who'd hired Camille and me was forced to step down. I decided to support the only other female full-professor than Camille to replace him. She was extremely grateful for my early and enthusiastic backing. I was rewarded by being appointed Director of Undergraduate Studies (DUS) that reduced my teaching load by one course. It soon became apparent that my philosophy of being an advocate for the undergraduates was not compatible with that of the chair who wanted a protector of the faculty. I also became aware that she was a very troubled and vengeful person suffering from a massive negative mother-complex. As Jung (1968) observed, such women suffer from "hypertrophy of the maternal element" resulting in a "ruthless will to power" (pp. 87–88). Consequently, at the end of my first year in this position, I offered to resign. The chair persuaded me to stay on.

The next year, an undergraduate I knew informed me that she had filed a sexual harassment complaint with the university against a graduate student in psychology who'd lowered her grade from an A to a B when she refused to date him. It was a clear violation of the university dating policy, and the graduate student readily confessed to me in writing to having done so. I informed the graduate student that, as DUS, I would recommend that he no longer be allowed to teach undergraduate courses. Soon thereafter, his mentor, arguably the most senior and famous member of our faculty, appeared menacingly at my office door. He was irate about my proposed action; after all, he said, "Boys will be boys," and "I need him as my teaching assistant to run my courses." He left, snarling, "I'll get you fired for this." And he did, since he was also the mentor of the chair. Normally, that would have been it, but this chair, like Nixon, kept an enemies list, and now I was on it. And, as Jung (1968, 88) predicted, such women "often succeed in annihilating not only their own personality but also the personal lives of their children" or those under their power.

The chair then pushed through a very divisive "workload" policy. Under it, most of the faculty would have their teaching load reduced from four to three courses per year with the minority, who were deemed not as productive, assigned to teach those extra courses. I could see my punishment coming and worked tirelessly to defeat this policy. Finally, the vote was held. I had counted carefully and thought it would be defeated by one vote, but it was a tie. Unfortunately, the chair got to cast the tie-breaking vote. A three-man committee was then appointed to review each faculty member's productivity and assign their course load.

I was called before this kangaroo-court tribunal. The lead member said some faculty members were so unproductive that they should teach ten courses if it were allowed. In my case, he proposed the slightly less draconian punishment of six courses! *Professor X, you seemed to gloat in the power and the punishment you could dispense.* I felt sick and humiliated. I had been very productive—still meeting the minimum acceptable criterion of two peer-reviewed publications per year, serving on various committees, and getting above average course evaluations. I did not see myself as "dead wood," but felt I was being treated that way. Fortunately, I had a research leave owed to me as compensation for the sabbatical I'd forgone to become DUS. This delayed the punishment.

During that time, the chair was up for reappointment, and I mobilized my colleagues to have her replaced. When informed that such significant opposition would prevent her from being reappointed, she left to become dean at a New York–area college. I naively thought that would be the end of the workload policy, but fate knocked once again.

While the next chair agreed that the policy was unfair, he decided to keep the three-course teaching load for the majority and have the unlucky seven teach four courses per year. The stigma was not to be removed. He even came to my office in an attempt to persuade me to teach the department's entire allotment of six sections of an Introduction to the University at Stony Brook, USB 101, a one-credit course that SBU had mandated for all incoming freshman, but that would not count against one's teaching requirement. As DUS, I had opposed the course as worthless and a drain on the faculty's time, and now I adamantly refused to teach more than the one section normally required of a faculty member. The students in my USB 101 class felt the same way about the class, and we all agreed not to meet.

One by one, those tarred with the scarlet letter *U* for unproductive decided to retire until only two others and I remained. Those two somehow had their penalty rescinded. I felt isolated and alone in my constant humiliation. It was like having to mourn my own death. After that chair retired, I then asked his successor, an extremely authoritarian, right wing person, what I could do. He barked, "Get a grant!" I had paid at least half my salary from grants for twenty-two years before coming to SBU, starting as an assistant professor at Duke University in 1969 and continuing at Northwestern University and the University of Michigan, Ann Arbor. And I even had some support during my first two years at SBU. So, I tried once again. First, I submitted a proposal twice to the American Cancer Society and then later to the National Institutes of Health. I almost succeeded, but the limited funds then available for social science research soon made it clear that it was not going to happen.

It was during this time that I entered "my year of death" (see chapter 4, Loss) and finally realized that academe was no longer where I needed to be. So I approached the dean about retirement and negotiated a deal that would allow me to retire at the end of the 2001–2002 academic year, when I would be 62 and could start Social Security. I was even awarded a retirement leave for the spring 2001 semester with no responsibilities, the last one ever given to SBU faculty.

At that point, I decided to heed the advice of a junior colleague (Professor Y) and announce my intention to retire at the end of the following academic year. That was the final blow that fate had in store for me. This colleague had been Camille's first hire, and we both considered her to be supportive as we had been of her. But it was she whose vote I had miscounted on the workload policy, and it was she, like a spoiled brat full of entitlement and devoid of empathy ("I'm doing it out of self-interest"), who'd cast the deciding vote for it.

In the fall of 2000, I had eleven students enrolled in a required graduate course, which I had labored, with the advice of this colleague and others in my area, to improve. Nevertheless, one by one she and another colleague whom I considered a good friend (*Professor Z, sometimes the tunnel vision of work can cast a shadow over close relationships*) pulled, pressured, and permitted their students to withdraw. It was like a Greek funeral with one's prized possessions, my remaining shreds of dignity, removed before the actual death. *O, Y that I could have shared half the suffering with you.*

Finally, I was down to just one student—a nonmatriculating person who was notorious for causing trouble. The chair, in a rare moment of magnanimity, said he would allow me to teach the course to this student. I declined and requested that my retirement begin immediately. This young colleague then came by my office to beg me to offer my graduate course in meta-analysis the following spring since she wanted to take it! After a moment of jaw-dropping disbelief, I told her firmly that my decision to retire cold turkey was unalterable.

And so it came to pass that I retired a full semester early. However, the dean, in a final gesture of goodwill, cushioned the salary loss by keeping me on the payroll until mid-October 2001. And I must say, in all candor, that so far, I've lived "happily ever after."

Epilogue. Both Jung and Nietzsche say that we must either embrace our fate, *amor fati,* or be drawn kicking and screaming to it. During the fall of 1998, I had gone on a healing trip to Greece to recover from all the death I had experienced (see chapter 4). Our trip leader was a therapist who took us to an ancient healing site where the Greeks of antiquity had constructed dream chambers. He hoped to replicate that experience. And it worked for me. While there, the following dream occurred.

Healing Dream

I drive through a street that resembles the white-tiled corridor of a hospital. The driver is an unfamiliar dark figure. Behind us is a faculty colleague riding a motorbike [Professor X]. This faculty member wounded me deeply a few years earlier [as head of the Work-Load Committee]. I remember saying, "he didn't have a soul." Suddenly, I notice the motorbike slide out of control, sending this professor sprawling across the pavement. I tell the driver to stop so we can help. He says someone behind us will come to the rescue. I scream, "This is a colleague. We've got to stop and help!" We stop. As I approach the body, I am overwhelmed with powerful feelings of distress. I cry out, "No more death! We need help! Is there a doctor?" Then I notice a vague white form over my colleague's body. I hear the voice of the doctor respond, "He'll be all right. It looks a lot worse than it is."
(Reprinted with permission from Tick 2001, 198)

The message from the dream was clear. My unconscious was sending a compensating signal (according to Jung) that I must not succumb to the ancient Greek cycle of betrayal, anger, and revenge. The dark figure, as in Jung's famous dream where he's carrying a "tiny light" on a dark, windy, foggy night and turns and sees "a gigantic black figure" (Jung 1989, 88), is my "shadow," or repressed unconscious, unwanted, mostly negative, character-istics. Perhaps X, Y, and Z will figure out who they are, reflect on their actions without the defensiveness of being named, and maybe even change themselves. That is all one can wish.

The dream had been accompanied by the release from se-vere pain caused by a stiff neck. It indicated that I needed no longer to be stiff-necked about my victimization which is often the case when one embraces or, as the Jungian Robert John-son (1993, 17) put it, "owns one's own shadow." And what better place to have such a dream than in Greece where the mythic archetypes, or "preexistent" and "primordial image[s]" (Jung 1968, 75), those Platonic forms of antiquity, are still alive in what Jung called the "collective unconscious," the "founda-tions of cultural history...beneath the personal psyche" (Jung 1989, 161). I could, as I did, mourn my loss and finally feel liber-ated, even reborn, from it.

Fate actually had something better in store for me. The be-ginning of my journey with Jung allowed me to put all the jigsaw pieces of my life together into a coherent and healing whole. These memoirs, including dreams and poems, will allow you, too, to embrace your fate in a meaningful and satisfying manner, especially if you are retired and have the time to engage in your own inner journey with Jung.

1 Childhood Influences

I Remember Fanny

I am the light of the world; whosoever follows me will never walk in darkness but will have a light which gives life.

—John 8:12

October 4, 2007, was the fiftieth anniversary of Sputnik, the Russian space satellite that shocked the United States by being the first man-made object to orbit the earth. My maternal grandmother, Fanny, who was visiting us (in Hartford, Connecticut) at the time of Sputnik's launch, wistfully recalled that it reminded her of her long-forgotten native Russian language. Fanny had emigrated from the Jewish Pale in eastern Poland and western Russia over a half century earlier. She told me that *sputnik* meant "satellite." Fanny was the only grandmother I really knew. My father's mother, Lena, simply known as *The Bubby* (Yiddish for *grandmother*), had removed herself from my life at the age of six.

It occurred after The Bubby had called me into her austere, foreboding presence to give me a pat on the head and a gift of the traditional Chanukah *gelt* (or money)—two shiny silver dollars. Shortly thereafter, my mother and father had a major, and soon to be recurrent, argument where she accused Lena of skimming money from the daily proceeds of the grocery business, which my father dutifully had her count each evening on his way home. It was not long before I was summoned to see The Bubby and to bring my gelt with me. My aunt Claire escorted me into her presence. The Bubby, with her piercing gray eyes; aging, pale skin; and frizzy white hair reminded me of the Wizard of Oz. She promptly announced (probably denounced) in a stern, hissing whisper of nearly incomprehensible Yiddish, translated by Claire, that she was taking back the gelt due to my *farstunkene* (literally "stinky," but here "stinker of a") mother's accusations. *Oy vey!* And, unlike Dorothy, I had forgotten to bring a pail of water with me. Although she lived only three blocks from my home, it might as well have been in Kansas for it was the last I ever saw of The Bubby.

My connection with Fanny was much more positive. I first remember visiting her when I was a little over three years old. My mother, who was about to give birth to my brother Ron, had sent me to Springfield, Massachusetts, to stay with Fanny during September and October of 1943. My major recollections were seeing ice delivered to her icebox, going to the little candy store around the block when I was good and Fanny gave me a nickel to spend, and meeting a strange and scary, very old lady. She was called "Little Bubby" and was Fanny's mother. She was supposedly over one hundred years old. Since she was blind, she wanted to touch me, but I was at first terrified of this little, gnome-like person. Sensing my discomfort, Fanny calmly put me at ease with words and by sitting next to me.

A few years later, when I was in second grade, Fanny was staying at our home while my mother was away. It was a rainy day and I put on my galoshes and walked the two blocks to the Sarah J. Rawson Elementary School. Once in my ground-floor classroom, I removed my galoshes, as always, by pulling down the back edge of one by using the front foot of the other and then shaking it completely off. This day, the right one seemed to stick and required considerable extra effort to shake loose. As I gave it a strong forward kick, it came loose and to my consternation flew high in the air like a missile. I stood transfixed as it soared above the desks toward the huge, tall windows on the other side of the room. Onward it went until it crashed into the very top of the farthest window and smashed through it. Fearing the awful consequences, I panicked and ran out of the building and all the way home where I hid under my bed.

It was there that Fanny found me and gently coaxed me out. After some milk and cookies, she once again reassured me that I shouldn't be afraid—that I should go back to school and that it would be all right. So I returned to find the janitor already repairing the broken window. He, too, was pleasant and only admonished me to be careful from now on when removing my galoshes.

My childhood was filled with many other visits to Springfield to see Fanny and her husband, my *zeyde* (or grandfather), Robert. And, I remember anticipating their arrival in their shiny, green Pontiac when they visited us on Holcomb Street. Sputnik marked Fanny's last visit there. The next year I left for college and our house was sold. Within two years, Zeyde died suddenly from a stroke, and Fanny began to show the first signs of Alzheimer's disease, which would later claim my mother. Fanny's visits ended and she became the ward of a cousin in Springfield. I saw her briefly a few more times as she slipped into dementia. One day, my mother called and casually mentioned that Fanny had died a few weeks earlier. By then I was away completing my graduate studies, and she thought I was too busy to be bothered. But I remember Fanny and how she constantly lifted me out of the darkness of fear.

As he claimed for his childhood maid, Jung (1989, 8) would say that, for me, Fanny was a positive feminine, or anima (the male's feminine aspect) influence on me. This would be in stark contrast to both The Bubby and my mother, Julia, who cast a very negative, even narcissistic, mother complex over me (see "Sh*t Happens!" in chapter 7). Such mothers demand that their children constantly strive to please them, thereby instilling in their children a fragile perfectionism as they desperately seek their mother's reluctant anima energy (see My Sinful Youth, or the Margaret Kennedy Affair section in this chapter). The desire for perfection can extend into parenting as I tried to be the perfect, overly protective parent. The resolution to the (anima mother) complex may come years later as it did for me (see Karin in chapter 8).

Fanny and Robert Mushnitsky

D-Day

Where love stops, power begins, and violence, and terror.

—C.G. Jung (2006, 103)

June 6 is the anniversary of D-Day—the day in 1944 when the Allies landed in Normandy and the final phase of World War II (WWII) began. It comes a bit more than a week after the original D-Day, as in Decoration Day, now renamed as Memorial Day. It is, unfortunately, celebrated as the unofficial start of summer with its three Bs—beaches, barbecues, and bikinis. A friend sent me, as a reminder of the war dead, one of Whitman's memorable Civil War poems—the war that Decoration Day commemorates, and the day when we are supposed to visit and decorate the graves of our fallen fathers, brothers and uncles. Sadly, mothers, sisters, and aunts are now joining them as women die in the wars in Afghanistan and Iraq.

On this day, I think of my uncles—Charlie, Jack, and Mack. All fought in WWII. D-Day was a week before my fourth birthday, yet I clearly remember my uncle Jack, who died in action five months earlier. He is one of my first memories, perhaps because he was a loving masculine or, as Jung would say, animus figure (see the following poem) that I, like all children, need but did not have in my father, Max, whose absence and anger kept that animus energy from me (see chapter 5, Facing the Father-Complex). And then Charlie and Mack returned from the war. Mack never spoke about it, but Charlie did. He was one of the top navigators in the Air Force and flew with Truman and MacArthur all over the world. I remember being six-years old and my eyes bugging out as he showed me the currencies he'd collected on all his wartime travels. He told me that in China, where he met Chiang Kai-shek, they still practiced infanticide and the Yangtze River was filled with drowned infants. Charlie was the true all-American, happy warrior, ever smiling and always your friend. He passed away in 2005.

I remember that the last Civil War veteran died around the time Charlie showed me the foreign money, and a decade later reading William Shirer's (1960) book *The Rise and Fall of the Third Reich*, which described the brutality of the concentration camps, where half of my grandmother Fanny's family had perished. There were gruesome photos, too, of open pits filled with bodies that I've never forgotten.

When I was sixteen, I got a summer job cleaning oil burners. All the guys I worked with were WWII veterans. They spoke of the war. I remember one saying how he had to "stack up bodies like cordwood" after the battle of Peleliu in the Pacific theater. I thought it strange that they would often go into the living rooms of the houses, open the bar, and take a shot of hard liquor. Now I understand.

I haven't decorated Charlie's or Jack's graves because I don't know where they are buried. But they have decorated my memories, as the following poem attests.

The Potato Chip Man

I've always had a passion for potato chips.
Is it some nervous addiction,
or a celebration of a smooth, round, salty treat
like some happy childhood memory that is
still crisp despite the years?

A small boy answers the snappy knock on the door.
A smile and a hand descend from the heavens
holding a tiny miracle—a 5-cent bag of
State Line potato chips.
Shazam! Uncle Jack in his pressed khaki uniform
is Captain Marvelous.

A year, a war, a holocaust, a childhood
goes screaming by.
A little boy stands uneasily before a stern
poster of Eisenhower in kindergarten.
Uncle Jack was killed at Anzio, shot by the Nazis
after fleeing Germany eight years earlier.
The bastards! On the home front there is no
armistice in the unrelenting parental warfare.

Now, have I grown old and brittle,
ready to snap with the next crunch of life
like some old salt who's been worn razor-thin
from voyages through the tumultuous seas of life?

And still I am a muncher of chips,
savoring their crisp taste,
gently sprinkled with salty tears.
And I remember that day as yesterday,
today, and tomorrow
when love descended from the sky
in a 5-cent bag of State Line potato chips.

You're an INFP

I was a late bloomer. But anyone who blooms at all, ever, is very lucky.

—Sharon Olds

That's what the report from http://haleonline.com/psychtest/ said. It's a website that performs a short version of Jung's personality typology (Jung, 1991) called the Myers-Briggs Type Indicator (MBTI). It is "the most widely used instrument in the world for determining personality," if you believe the hype on the dust jacket (see Myers and Myers, 1980). One of my college classmates recommended it to me in a recent e-mail. For only $0.99, you'll find out who you are. So who am I?

Well, Jung is famous for having coined the terms *introversion* and *extraversion*, or our orientation toward the world. Are we outward looking focusing on the "outer world of people and things," an extravert (or an "E" according to the MBTI), or inward looking, more absorbed in our "inner world of concepts and ideas," an introvert (or "I" in this system). I'm an I, which means I have to work hard to relate to others. According to the MBTI, I have an auxiliary or helping function, my *intuition*, or "N"—as opposed to those who gather their information primarily through their senses, "S" for Sensing types—which is how I deal with the outer world.

The biggest surprise for me, a retired psychology professor, was that my primary way of evaluating information was as a Feeling type (or "F") as opposed to the expected Thinking (or "T") type. I had dedicated my professional life to scientific research. Why, just a few years ago, I had even written the following poem describing a critical moment in my early development that was all about thinking.

Connecticut Derby, or How I Found My Brain

I had a horse when I was young.
It was in second grade, and
he was a black stallion.
OK, he was only made
of paper that our teacher,
Mrs. Beers, with her plump,
grandmotherly figure complete
with graying hair bun and
glasses hanging by a necklace
on a bosom substantial enough
to nurture an entire class,
had us draw and cut out.
But I had seen the pictures and
knew fast horses had all
their hooves off the ground.
Yes, I knew they flew and
that was how my horse looked.

Then Mrs. Beers, with her
ever present knowing smile,
had them all lined up
just above the blackboard
on the right and she said,
"Your horse is only
as fast as your brain.
Every time you learn something
your horse will move ahead."
Well, I wasn't so sure
about the "brain" thing.
My angry father always scolded me,
"You have too much mouth and
too little brain for your own good."

Well, sure enough,
Hank's and Billy's steeds
jumped way ahead.
They were the two
class geniuses who'd soon
skip the next grade
and disappear into
the cloud of memory.
My horse just kept
lingering at the starting gate
while everyone else's brain
joined the learning chase.
But my mother kept reading
the comics with me and
my grandma had me adding
up the points as she
trounced me in gin rummy.

And soon my sleek stallion
bolted forward like Whirlaway,
and there was no one
who was going to stop him.
Over the weeks and months,
he flew forward, overtaking
the others one by one.
In the late-spring homestretch
Hank's and Billy's mounts were ahead
by just a few subtraction exercises, and
when the last bell of school rang,
my horse won—"by a nose!"
Then I knew I had a brain;
I had the horse to prove it.

So what happened? Was I a fake "T" after all these years?
Then the proverbial "sky opened up" and I had one of those
eureka experiences. I really was an "F," but I had to go

undercover to get through my childhood where my home had been a constant battleground with my parents engaged in hand-to-hand, insult-to-insult combat. My emotions were rubbed raw, and I had to retreat. Becoming a little thinking smarty not only saved my feeling self, which was pretty numb by then, but had also gotten me some needed parental praise, especially from my mother, that made survival possible. As Jung (1968, 91) said, "resistance to the mother can sometimes result in a spontaneous development of intellect for the purpose of creating a sphere of interest in which the mother has no place." While Jung was referring to daughters and mothers, it clearly can work for sons as well.

Even when I finally escaped to college, I thought I'd be an engineer—a very thinking career. But I was somewhat ambivalent. My mother, to her credit, figured this out (but see the Afterword). Without asking me, she turned down my full scholarship to Rensselaer Polytechnic Institute and sent in my acceptance to Yale, the only liberal arts college I'd been admitted to. While I was thrilled to be attending an Ivy League school, I still believed I was a "T" type and decided to major in mathematics, despite all the evidence to the contrary. Luckily, the new field of computer science was emerging, and I was allowed to take a course in computer applications that counted toward my major. I was hooked by programs that played chess and did other "intelligent," or thinking, tasks.

I then applied to graduate school in computer science and was admitted to my top choice, Carnegie Institute of Technology, soon to become Carnegie Mellon University. There I transferred into psychology and worked with the future Nobel laureate Herbert Simon and his alter ego, Allen Newell, on computer simulation of human thinking. So, I still was following the path of a T type. Then those first F-type doubts entered my mind. I began asking myself, "What about emotions?" They seemed so essential but were considered totally unimportant to Professor Simon, the ultimate thinking intellect, who called emotions "interrupts."

So what happened? Once I started my career, my F type–feeling side slowly began to emerge. By the time, my wife obtained her PhD, I was ready to switch to an area more consistent with my true self. Fortunately, we were both offered positions in psychology at Northwestern University, where I worked with another genius named Donald Campbell on the evaluation of social programs (see chapter 3, St. Don and the Beard). A key aspect differentiating F from T Types is a desire to "contribute to the welfare of society by their loyal support of good works and those movements, generally regarded as good by the community, which they feel correctly about and so can serve effectively" (Myers and Myers, 1980, fig. 26). This is what I was doing—using new scientific methods to determine whether innovative educational and health programs were effective (see the My Work sections in chapter 3). Nevertheless, I kept on believing that I was a Thinking type. The methods I specialized in focused on correcting errors in scientific inference. Of course, it was also a way to shore up one's thinking.

It wasn't until I came to Stony Brook University in 1990 and resumed writing poetry that my true F type finally became apparent. Poetry was how I could express my feeling side, which was ready to emerge with my entrance into the "second half of life," where it is "a duty and necessity to devote serious attention" to oneself (Jung 1969c, 398–99). Now I finally realized that it was not my brain, but my heart, that I'd found at last.

My Sinful Youth, or the Margaret Kennedy Affair

All the people about me seemed to take the jargon for granted...such as that God...created human beings so that they would have to sin, and nevertheless forbids them to sin and even punishes them by eternal damnation in hell-fire.

—**C. G. Jung (1989, 46)**

During the summer of 1947, my mother wanted to follow her girlfriends to the Connecticut shore to escape the heat and her husband. Of course, there was still the problem of what to do with us—her three boys, Ron, aged three; me, who recently turned seven; and Alan, ten—all affectionately referred to as "you rotten kids." Her solution was to bring along our regular babysitter, Margaret Kennedy, for the two weeks to supervise us while my mother played mah-jongg, canasta, and other such diversions with her female companions.

Margaret Kennedy is the only one of the series of babysitters we had who I remember. She was in her late teens; had shoulder-length, dark hair; and rosy, apple-colored cheeks. She was an observant Catholic who felt it part of her duties to take me to church with her on those occasions when she didn't have to care for my brothers. We would enter the imposing concrete monolith of St. Justin's church located on Blue Hills Avenue (in Hartford, Connecticut) about a mile from my house and immediately be enveloped in a soaring darkness penetrated by multicolored light that filtered through three, towering stained-glass windows. It was here amid the immense cavernous awe that, Margaret claimed, we must confront our sins if we were ever to get into heaven.

Of course, I wanted to go to heaven and be with all the good people. Margaret told me that St. Peter guarded the gate to heaven, where he had a book containing a record of all our sins and all our good deeds. I immediately started to keep my own record: not washing my hands on both sides—bad, and therefore a sin according to my grandma, Fanny. Fighting with my brothers was also bad and a major sin. Not cleaning my plate despite "all the starving people in China" added yet another sin. Not pleasing or obeying my mother—a seeming impossibility—was another biggie that was even mentioned in our very own Ten Commandments. "Why can't you be good like Stevie Pearson?" my mother always asked me. It was all overwhelming. The sins were adding up faster than my small efforts to be the "good son," by taking out the trash, cleaning the dishes, hanging the clothes on the line to dry, and mowing the lawn, could balance them. Heaven was out of the question. I was doomed; hell and eternal damnation would be my final destination.

And so our contentious band, minus my ever-absent father, arrived that July in a little duplex, beachfront cottage aptly named "Punch & Judy." I, the hapless sinner, was about to be the coconspirator in the major offense of my youth. My precocious older brother, Alan, perhaps anticipating puberty, had decided to investigate the physical charms of Margaret Kennedy. His plan, such as it was, involved hiding in her closet and observing her while she changed into her swimsuit. I was sworn to secrecy. However, I was not allowed in the closet, since Alan, the control freak anointed by primogeniture, reserved that leading-man privilege, as he had with all the plays he wrote, directed, and produced a few years earlier, solely for himself. Well, the plan was a fiasco! Alan was discovered, and all hell broke loose.

All I remember is hearing a very loud scream—as, it turned out, when Margaret opened her closet to hang up her clothes—and considerable commotion. The next thing I knew, Margaret had left for good, soon to be followed by Alan, who was temporarily exiled to an overnight camp without ever revealing to me her charms (or lack thereof). My mother receded further into her narcissistic card playing with her female friends.

The penance fate assigned me was to patrol the empty, endless purgatory of the Connecticut shore, where the tide always seemed low no matter how far out into the water I walked. It was here among the foot-piercing debris of innumerable broken shells and peeling swatches of sunburnt skin that I formed a lasting dislike for Long Island Sound. But that vast, fiery expanse also bleached out my memory of Margaret Kennedy, along with the fear of heaven, hell, and the need to keep score of the good and evil that had plagued my heretofore sinful youth. Like Jung's youthful experience at the cathedral (see chapter 5, Sh*t Happens!), I, too, felt an enormous, an indescribable relief. I, unlike Jung, could now return to my equally flawed Old Testament God, who said, "I form the light and create darkness; I make peace and create evil; I the Lord do all these things" (Isaiah 45:7).

Water Torture

None of us stands outside humanity's black collective shadow.

—C.G. Jung (2006, 95)

It seems like such a very long time ago, but it's only been a few years. Before Bear Stearns, before Lehman Brothers, before A.I.G.; before subprime mortgages, derivatives, credit default swaps; before the whole worldwide financial collapse and the economic torture bequeathed to us by George W. Bush, there was rendition to so-called dark sites, where medieval versions of the rack were reenacted anew under the euphemism of "water boarding." We were reminded of this by Darth ("We may have to go to the dark side") Cheney who reemerged from an undisclosed location to warn us on how unsafe we all are without torture. I was so troubled by our national descent into brutality that I'd written the following letter for *The Times*:

To the Editor:

My heart screams out, "Shame on us!"

Ironically, it is the new German chancellor who has to counter our secretary of state about "rendition," which is clearly newspeak for torture.

I will bear witness to this descent into madness, refuse to condone it, will seek to redress it and hold all our elected officials accountable.

I refuse to be a willing accomplice.

Published by *The New York Times*, December 8, 2005

As a psychologist, I wondered if there was more to my intense reaction to torture than my conscious Jewish identity with its Holocaust sensitivity. A discussion in one of my retirement-group classes unearthed the buried memories. It took me back (where else) to my childhood when, as Jung predicted, a similar emotion-laden event occurred. As Jung (1985, 230) noted, "[It] is indeed the infantile channel along which the libido [or psychic energy] flows back when it encounters any obstacles in later years, thus reactivating the long-forgotten psychic contents of childhood." I was in first grade and hating every minute of it. One day I told my mother, Julia, that I didn't feel well enough to go to school. "Oh, you poor thing," she said. "Let me feel your keppie." Then I noticed a gleam in her eye as she directed, "Follow me; I've got just the cure you need." And with those innocent words, my rendition began.

Up the stairs we went, entering the dark site of our communal bathroom. My mother reached into the shower and lifted out the mysterious red rubber bag with the long, thin snakelike hose attached to one end. She then turned on the warm water faucet. "What's that for?" I asked with a bit of trepidation creeping into my voice.

"Don't worry!" she exclaimed calmly. "I use this all the time, and it makes me feel better."

"What's it called, and how does it work?" I asked with increasing suspicion and panic.

"It's called an enema," she replied and proceeded to explain how it worked.

"No, no!" I exclaimed. And like most prisoners I begged, "Don't do it." But there was still that glint in her eye. "All right, all right, I confess. I didn't want to go to school, but I'm really not that sick." But it was too late. Despite my squirming, the snake found that unmentionable place (now a common curse word probably favored by former enema abusers), and the bag deflated as my intestines inflated to near bursting.

A few decades later, I would study the controversy about "one-trial learning," but I already was convinced that it was true. It had only taken one enema to convince me of that. Every time my mother would look at me a say, "Paul, your face is flushed. Are you sick?" I was ready with a response before she could get that gleam in her eye.

"Oh, no," I'd shoot back. "I was just in the sun too long."

Now I've reached that time in life often revered as a "second childhood" where we get to reenact all the fun things from our youth with our grandchildren. But, as Jung and Cheney would predict, there is a dark or shadow side as well. I learned this during an annual visit to my Greek goddess physician, Dr. A (for Augoustiniatos), who is a truly caring and gifted healer, in the tradition of her ancestor, Hippocrates. As she examined my computerized medical history with her usual thoroughness, I noticed an impish gleam come into her eye. She turned to me and said, "You need to schedule a colonoscopy." I had to rub my eyes for a second as I thought I saw and heard Julia Wortman.

2 Marriage

I Was Married by the ACLU

When...the individual becomes [a] social unit and the State is elevated to the supreme principle, it is only to be expected that the religious function too will be sucked into the maelstrom.

—C.G. Jung (2006, 24)

I know you're thinking, "How can the American Civil Liberties Union (ACLU) be involved with marriage? That has nothing to do with The Bill of Rights." Well, the conventional wisdom is often wrong, so please bear with me if I digress to another instance of such a failing of the conventional wisdom.

We all know that there is supposed to be a separation of church and state. That, too, is part of our civic canon of conventional wisdom. While technically right on the federal level (but don't get me going about Republicans and Christian fundamentalism), it does not apply to the states, especially those few designated as commonwealths. One such state is Pennsylvania founded and named after the Quaker William Penn.

Back in the turbulent 1960s, I was a graduate student at Carnegie Mellon University (CMU) in Pittsburgh, Pennsylvania.

A young assistant professor there who had recently married a CMU undergrad informed me that the Commonwealth of Pennsylvania allows any resident to be married using the Quaker service. Essentially, that means there's no formal priesthood or rabbinate involved, and the ceremony is, more or less, a do-it-yourself marriage.

The information about the availability of the Quaker service spread quickly among my fellow graduate students. It was especially appealing to those longhaired, pot-smoking, countercultural types who were engaged in nontraditional relationships. In short, almost all of us! I, myself, a so-called NJB, or "nice Jewish boy," was engaged to an undergraduate student, Camille Badzgon, from a very conservative, Lutheran household.

I had been introduced to Camille at a Vietnam War protest rally organized in the fall of 1965 by a mutual friend. Camille looked as if she'd stepped through time as the physical manifestation of my awkward grade-school drawings of young women. She was, as Jung would say, a true anima figure, or my inner, unconscious ideal version of the feminine. But I, at the exalted age of twenty-five, felt she was too young. Fortunately for me, Camille did not feel that way and sought me out on numerous occasions, first in asking me to become a contributor to the campus newspaper opposing the war and later as a volunteer subject in one my dissertation studies. Her timing could not have been more perfect. As my relationship with the seductive Yvonne evaporated, I finally became fully aware of Camille.

How lucky it was for me. For while Yvonne was my mother incarnate—in looks, personality, and cultural background, Camille was my antimother—just the type of person Jung would recommend. She was attentive, caring, self-actualizing, and smart. It was, on the surface, a case of "opposites attract," but what I learned as the years went by was that we each had buried in our unconscious identical mother and father complexes. That bond may have been the hidden force that united us and kept us together as we provided the mutual support needed to uncover and confront those complexes. As Jung (1968, 99) said about women like Camille, with negative mother-complexes, "This rare combination of womanliness and masculine understanding proves invaluable in the realm of intimate relationships...Owing to her qualities...men often favor her with the projection of positive mother-complexes."

After a truly whirlwind romance, we moved in together and shortly thereafter decided to marry upon the completion of my dissertation. We believed the Quaker service would be the best way of handling the religious issue that divided our families if not us. With this ceremony in mind, Camille and I set a date to be married for late August 1967 and sent out wedding invitations. We then went downtown to obtain our marriage license. We were stunned when it was denied. The clerk informed us that he was not going to issue another license to "you CMU hippies." He was incensed that just the week before one of my colleagues had applied. He was white and his fiancée was black. So, we asked if we could appeal and were told that the judge was "on vacation" and would not return until after our scheduled wedding day. What were we to do?

OK, so you probably figured out that this is where the ACLU comes in. And you're absolutely correct. As Vietnam War protesters, we were not about to let a small-minded government bureaucrat prevent us from being legally married under the laws available to all Pennsylvanians. It was then that I suggested we contact the ACLU. The local director, Marjorie Mattson, had made quite a name for herself in a recent campaign to become district attorney. Ms. Mattson herself returned my call and quickly informed me that there was no legal basis for denying our marriage license. One phone call from her resolved the issue, and the license was ours.

With a $200 budget and seventy-five guests, the marriage ceremony was held on August 26 in the CMU chapel. Camille's former boyfriend provided the entertainment. He played the harpsichord loaned to us by the professor who'd first told us about the Quaker service. Camille and I read the vows we composed and married one another.

So, now you know why I'm a lifelong ACLU member. Even when most American Jews abandoned the ACLU because they supported George Lincoln Rockwell's American Nazi Party march through Skokie, Illinois, I did not. After all, they're pro-family, pro-marriage, and will defend individuals against the inappropriate use of state power. And that, too, defies the conventional wisdom. As Jung (2006, 102) wisely observed, "The question of human relationship and the inner cohesion of our society is an urgent one in view of the atomization of the pent-up mass man, whose personal relationships are undermined by general mistrust." And there is no more fundamental relationship essential to social cohesion than marriage, which, even today, is denied to many through the fearful projections of the "mass man."

The Seven-Year Itch

We rush impetuously into novelty, driven by a mounting sense of insufficiency, dissatisfaction, and restlessness.

—C.G. Jung (1989, 236)

I was in the kitchen on the phone with a Northwestern colleague when suddenly I saw someone speed past, which was followed by a tremendous crash.

"What the hell was that?" he asked.

"You won't believe this, but my wife just skated by on her new in-line Rollerblades and landed in the dishwasher. I'll have to call you back."

I hung up and raced over to Camille to see how she was doing. The dishwasher was open since I hadn't finished loading it when the phone rang. Luckily, I'm one of those compulsive dishwasher loaders who always put the knives in blade down.

"Honey, are you all right?" I asked as I reached to help her up.

"I'm fine," she responded, "but I'm not sure about my future as a skater."

"Well, maybe there's something else you'd find interesting," I blurted out, unaware of the consequences.

"Sweetheart, you know, I've been thinking that we really should do something together," she immediately answered as if anticipating the suggestion.

"What do you have in mind?" I asked with some trepidation knowing Camille to be a first-class sensation seeker, while I was a first-class introvert and sensation avoider.

"I think we should learn to scuba dive," she said with that adventurous gleam in her eye.

"Scuba dive! Are you crazy?" I replied incredulously as panic enveloped me.

"Honey, you've got to admit that it's a bit boring here dealing with these confining Chicago winters. We've been married seven years and it's time we tried something new, something completely different."

"But I don't know if I can handle that," I pleaded in vain.

"Well, if this marriage is going to survive, you're just going to have to try," she said with a firmness that indicated finality.

So, for the next twelve weeks, we trudged the two blocks through the snow to the Northwestern University pool. The outside temperature was 10 degrees, and inside, the pool was kept at a balmy 60 degrees. Lou, from the local dive shop, gave us lectures and then exercises in the pool. It all culminated with a written test and then the ultimate underwater trial by Chinese water torture. Starting from the shallow end of the pool, one had to swim its Olympic-regulation length of seventy-five feet underwater to the deep end. There at the bottom was a pile of scuba gear. Our task was to get there and put all the gear on—regulator, tank, mask, fins, and weight belt.

Amazingly, I passed. Lou cheerfully congratulated us, proclaiming, "You're now certified to scuba dive in any pool in the country." But before I could get comfortable with the thought that now I could return to other pursuits, Camille informed me that, as a reward, we were going on Lou's dive trip to Roatan Island in Honduras during spring break!

We arrived in Honduras and passed our checkout dive test held in the shallow waters off the beach. We then retired to dinner, where the choice was either lobster or pork. All the natives opted for pork while we chose the lobster. The next morning, Camille was writhing in pain. The tourista had struck her. Her intestines seemed to be her only point of vulnerability, and mine were one of my few strengths. Another example, perhaps, of the Jungian balance one finds in relationships.

"It's OK, honey," she said. "Go ahead and enjoy the dive." I wasn't sure if she was joking, but off I went in a show of false bravery.

I soon learned that we were going to visit something known as the Eel Garden. Evidently, these particular eels look like green weeds protruding from the ocean floor. If you're quiet, you can creep up on them. But, once they spot you, they disappear into the sand. Not the most exciting natural phenomenon, but seemingly innocuous I thought. At least until I learned that the eel garden was a 112 feet down! At that point, like some condemned man, I started to engage the instructor in bargaining. "Couldn't I just go down thirty or forty feet and watch?" I begged.

"No," he said, "It wouldn't be safe."

So, I decided to stay five feet behind the dive guide and follow his feet down. And it worked. I was even able to equalize pressure to keep my ears from imploding. And, as predicted, the eels promptly vanished once they spotted us. As it turned out, so did my wedding band.

And then it was time to go back to the surface. Of course, it's not so simple at that depth. You have to stop periodically as you ascend to let the gases work their way out to avoid the bends. Well, just as my tank read empty, I got the thumbs-up to head to the surface.

There is a psychological theory called *opponent processes*, which predicts that when one strong emotion is unnecessary its opposite emotion or "opponent process" will kick in. Very Jungian it seemed. And that's just what happened. Upon returning to the surface, the immense fear was unneeded and in rushed an incredible feeling best described as ecstasy. At that point, I was ready to try skydiving.

Epilogue. Camille eventually recovered but missed all of the deepest dives, such as the truly epic, panic-inducing Hole in the Wall at over two hundred feet down. I watched in astonishment as the dive guide's depth meter on his watch went from green, to yellow, to red.

Thirty years later, in the fall of 2005, my wife learned that she had a common heart defect called a PFO, or hole in the heart. The doctor asked her if she was a scuba diver. "Not anymore" she replied. "Is it a problem?"

"Yes" he said. "It can be fatal. And it's the only occupation that immediately qualifies you for corrective surgery."

"Thank God for tourista," I thought.

Christmas Tree Complexes

Complexes are like little children. We need to educate them, and let them grow up.

—M.-L. von Franz (Lecture by Armin Wanner, April 20, 2005)

In this troubled world, we know that religion is a continual cause of conflict. I'd thought this was something in my external world, outside of my immediate family. I grew up in a Jewish home but soon became disillusioned with the overly hostile God of the Old Testament. He was too much like my father, who used to put "the fear of God" in me by chasing me with a butcher knife. So after my bar mitzvah, I walked out of the synagogue and have rarely returned.

My religious, anything-but-my-father, rebellion even extended to my choice of a spouse. My failed graduate school flirtation with the nubile Yvonne was the final proof I needed to embrace my loving shicksa Camille. She was an equally irreligious, non-congregational Lutheran. Religion was just not a central part of our lives until, after sixteen years of marriage, we had a baby. Suddenly this became an issue. In particular, the celebration of the major religious holidays like Christmas and Chanukah seemed very important.

Camille and I both agreed that we should celebrate both. That meant lighting candles for Chanukah and having a Christmas tree, which I affectionately called our Chanukah bush. I was left to my own devices for Chanukah, although Camille developed into a world-class latke maker. Of course, it's simple to buy a menorah—you only have to do it once—and to light candles and chant the prayers. The Christmas tree is quite another matter. Little did I realize that it would tap into some deeper psychological place, one that put Camille and me at odds.

Camille insisted that I participate in the Christmas ritual that involved buying, installing, and decorating the tree. I had no trouble with buying one, although I soon learned that height and a trimmed base were important. Decorating was also relatively easy, although tree lights are notoriously unreliable. It was installing the tree where something in the dark shadows of our personalities emerged and created havoc.

The first problem was transporting the tree into the living room and placing it in the stand. The initial wound seemed to be squeezing the tree through passageways that always seemed just a bit too tight. This had the effect of making us both anxious for the next, and often, fatal step of getting the tree in the stand. Somehow, the stand was always too small even though we now have a collection of four or five. This required some last-minute cutting. But where was the saw? Who knows? Did the workmen take it? My lack of handiness—my unhandy complex—would then kick in. My neighbor, a Jewish woman also in a mixed marriage, put it succinctly, "Of course, you're not handy; you're Jewish." At this point, I was in a very fragile state. Unfortunately, so was Camille.

It took me a while to realize that for her, Christmas had to be perfect, and my lack of calm handiness combined with the inevitably balky tree was just the imperfection that would set her off. Soon we'd be two psychotic individuals struggling to force the tree into its stand. Then we'd stand back to see if it was straight—both right to left and front to back. This seemed completely impossible, and we were soon simultaneously reduced to acrimonious blubbering. "A little to the right; now a bit left; *oy vey,* the top is crooked; who picked this pathetic tree with scoliosis anyway?"

Jung claims that women seek completeness while men strive for perfection. Not in our household, not with Camille and me. She is constantly seeking the perfect Christmas holiday that eluded her as a child while I'm trying for completeness in getting the bleeping tree into its hole and escaping from my unhandy complex. According to Jung, a complex is like a hurricane or tornado--a swirling emotionality surrounding a central archetypal core. For both of us, the archetype was a combination of the negative, or devouring, mother and the absent, hostile father who always scolded us for our imperfections. Camille wanted the love of a disapproving mother, and I wanted to avoid the criticism of an unappeasable father. Ah, the collision of two complexes is like star systems exploding into a supernova—a "terrible beauty is born" to quote the poet W. B. Yeats ("Easter, 1916"). We were like two marionettes controlled by hostile mothers lashing out at each other in blind emotion as we struggled with the tree.

Well, now that I've retired, Camille and I have declared a truce. I'm no longer allowed anywhere near the Christmas tree except to put presents under it. In fact, now that we are aware of the complex, its effect has greatly diminished. It never goes away, but once you're conscious of it, you rob it of its power. You can easily step back, realize what's at work, apologize for any momentary lapse, and move on.

My Fortieth Anniversary

And now abideth faith, hope, love, these three; but the greatest of these is love.

—I Corinthians 13, King James Bible

On August 26, 2007, Camille and I celebrated our fortieth wedding anniversary. We'd flown to Chicago to spend that weekend with my older son, Jer, and his wife, Katie. Our other son, Andrew, had flown there the day before. Jer had scripted the entire weekend with dinners at three different ethnic restaurants of our choice and an anniversary boat trip run by the Chicago Architecture Foundation on the Chicago River through the many notable, downtown skyscrapers.

But what do a husband and wife discuss on such a momentous day? Well, and this is hard for a Jungian to admit, we had an illuminating and—if you must know, titillating—early morning discussion of our sexual hang-ups! Okay, I've promised not to go into the specific details (sorry), but it turns out—and here Jung does get his due—which we both suffered from very similar mother complexes. Camille's mother was, to coin a term, de-feminating while mine was emasculating (see chapter 4, My Year of Death—Mother).

That was the attitude my mother, and her three sisters, had toward all men. I remember her youngest sister, Ida, complaining after a doctor's visit, "Can you believe it! He told me I had to give up bowling. Sex, I could understand, but bowling?" Well, men were not safe in my mother's family, which may have accounted for my fondness for her father, Robert, who was a kindly, good-natured man in a family, both lacking those qualities as well as a masculine presence that my father had abdicated. Such was my affection for poor, henpecked Bob, who fate blessed with four daughters and no sons, that, following the Jewish tradition, Jer's middle name is Robert.

So like Bob, there was no pleasing his daughter and my mother, Julia, no matter how perfect I tried to be. Camille suffered a similar fate as the constant reminder of her mother's failed marriage. She, too, aimed at perfection to both please and protect her from powerful adults. But her mother always kept the feminine for herself, both looking and dressing seductively until she died. There was no pleasing her either.

Camille and I could now see the complexed behavior our mothers had bequeathed us. And like guilty teenagers or newlyweds, we could finally celebrate our freedom from it. As Jung said about daughters with a negative mother complex (1968, 98), "The woman with this type of mother-complex probably has the best chance of all to make her marriage an outstanding success during the second half of life." So, we could at last enjoy ourselves fully in both body as well as mind without the specter of the disapproving mother.

Later that afternoon, Camille and Katie decided to go shopping. Katie was determined to capture the feminine for Camille, who'd lost twenty pounds and gone from a size 12 dress to a svelte size 8. Off they went to explore the shops on Chicago's Magnificent Mile. A few hours later, they returned with many bags in hand. My eyes were immediately drawn to the small, pink one labeled Victoria's Secret. Katie had been working hard to get Camille to abandon the boxy, masculine clothes she was accustomed to wearing for a more formfitting, feminine look. Tighter blouses from Macy's and slender pants from J. Crew emerged to demonstrate this new look.

Finally, Camille reached into the Victoria's Secret bag to reveal a very sexy bra. "Katie made me go in there against my will," she said sheepishly. "Then they insisted on measuring me, and guess what?" she added. "I'm not a size 40A, but a 36C!"

"That's wonderful," I replied thinking of the famous French maxim *vive la difference*.

That evening, we joined Jer and Andrew for our anniversary feast at Pegasus restaurant in Greektown. A large, boisterous street festival surrounded it. I grabbed Camille's hand, and like Zorba, I danced my way through the dense crowd and into the restaurant.

Once we were inside and seated, the conversation turned to Camille's shopping spree. As I started to mention Camille's newfound femininity at Victoria's Secret, both Jer and Andrew interrupted, saying in unison, "Dad, that's more information than we need." Andrew added, "Here, let me take a picture of you and Mom with your cell phone and make it your new background."

The author and his wife, Camille, at Pegasus

At that moment, the *saganaki* arrived, was anointed in oil, touched with a match, and burst into flames with the customary, "Oopah!" That was a fitting climax to our anniversary.

3 Career

Miss MM

Who knows what evil lurks in the hearts of men? The Shadow knows.

—The Shadow, radio drama

As a new and inexperienced assistant professor, I found Duke University both intimidating and difficult. I was self-conscious and extremely anxious when in the presence of my new and famous faculty associates who insisted on the daily ritual of lunch at the Duke Faculty Club. My graduate training, in what would emerge as the new field of cognitive psychology, was totally foreign to the traditional training and practice discussed by my older colleagues. So, I suffered through countless lunches, feeling inadequate and incompetent.

The work was not any easier. Carnegie Mellon, where I'd completed my doctoral research, was one of the top two academic computer facilities in the country, and now, I felt as though I'd returned to the Stone Age. Instead of remote data entry typing from a terminal, I had to keypunch cards, and instead of advanced programming languages, I had to obtain the IBM manuals and program in the binary (actual "hex") language of machine code. Fortunately, a friend from graduate school, Bobby Jo Caviness, had returned to his native state to join the faculty at the Duke Computer Center. He was able to guide me through some of the more obscure technobabble that characterized those manuals.

There I continued to refine a part of my thesis project involving the computer simulation of a neurologist performing clinical diagnoses. This was so time-consuming, given the primitive computing resources, that I realized I'd have to develop another research program in order to be viewed as productive—that is, publishing at least two peer-reviewed papers in reputable journals per year. Fortunately, my dissertation, focusing on the organization and structure of human memory, proved to be a gold mine, and I got four good publications from it. But I had no graduate students. Camille, who had more political street smarts than I did, soon discovered that my faculty colleagues in experimental psychology were conspiring to prevent me from getting any grad students. So I decided to work with talented undergraduates.

A young psychology major and marathon runner on the cross-country team named Phil Sparling approached me about lab work and we began a series of studies on long-term memory. Phil was perfect for such a project as he was used to hard work over long distances. He and I were both rewarded with publications in the leading journals in the field. Then he graduated and went on to pursue a career in medical research.

In the meantime, another undergraduate who I'll call Miss MM had sought me out. She also expressed an interest in my work. As it turned out, her most outstanding feature was her chest. She had the largest bosom I've ever seen, and she wasn't embarrassed about revealing her remarkable cleavage. I remember one early spring day her coming to my office and just slightly leaning toward the table. Her mammoth breasts were prominently displayed and were literally resting on the table a foot below. I glanced out my open office door, which faced the faculty lounge, and noticed my colleague—and "dirty old man" of the department, Cliff Wing—looking in. His eyes popped out at the sight, and he was so distracted that he missed the entrance to the lounge and walked into the wall. I tried vainly to stifle a laugh to the consternation of Miss MM.

She claimed to have come with an invitation to give a talk on my research work at her dormitory. Unsuspecting, I agreed and showed up one evening a couple of weeks later only to find no one, but Miss MM, there. She apologized for the confusion, claiming a scheduling error. Instead, she offered me a tour of her room that had been conveniently cleared of roommates. Suddenly, as I was escorted to her bed, it became clear that I was being offered more than a casual glimpse of Miss MM's magnificent mammaries. I panicked; said that Camille was expecting me for a late dinner; and left in a rush of embarrassment.

Meanwhile, Camille's faculty advisor, Jack Brehm, an eminent social psychologist, was busy pursuing her. When she said she liked photography, he joined her. I fumed as they went out on photo shoots and he persuaded her to develop film with him in the darkroom. But, as I had done with Miss MM, Camille managed to escape his lecherous advances. I was not so lucky with respect to Brehm. He somehow got himself appointed to my interim, two-year review committee along with another colleague, Norman Guttman, who was considered nonproductive or "dead wood." They composed two-thirds of the committee. Marty Lakin, a former Israeli freedom fighter and a supportive friend, was the third.

At the time, I had tried to get my undergrads to appreciate discrimination by reading an infamous article called "Student as Nigger" by Jerry Farber. It was filled with sexually explicit terms like *cunnilingus* and *fellatio*. Knowing my conservative, white audience, I warned them that they could skip it or have a friend read it, omitting the scatological terms. I was teaching that, as Jung said, "the white man carries a very heavy burden indeed. It shows us a picture of the common human shadow that could hardly be painted in blacker colors. The evil that comes to light in man and that undoubtedly dwells within him is of gigantic proportions" (2006, 94). So I was stunned when the shadow enveloped me.

The department chair called me in to inform me that a student had reportedly sent a copy of the article to the university's president. This didn't ring true, and I decided to ask my students about it. They said none of them had felt the need to do such a thing. Fortunately, I was on very good terms with the department secretaries. One of them soon approached me to say that Professor Guttman had asked her about the article when she was duplicating it. He had taken a copy. It was clear what had happened, and I informed the chair. Nevertheless, I was shocked when he called me in for the oft-postponed review meeting he'd evidently been avoiding and informed me that my contract was not being renewed. I felt as if I'd been shot. I stumbled upstairs to my office and broke down. The tears bled from my eyes and spattered on the rubble of the past eleven years—four at Yale, five at Carnegie Mellon, and then two at Duke—a career grievously, but, as it turned out, not mortally, wounded.

Epilogue. Thirty-two years later, just before I retired from Stony Brook University in 2001, I received both an e-mail and a written note. They were from Phil Sparling. He was now a Professor of Applied Physiology at Georgia Tech and had written an article on how he'd been inspired to pursue a research career. I had been the inspiration! It was one of the most gratifying moments of my career.

St. Don and the Beard

Science is timeless.

—D. T. Campbell

Donald T. Campbell

After Camille's graduation from Duke, we decided to remain there. Camille, who had not wanted to attend Duke, had been admitted to its graduate program in social psychology. Ironically, it turned out to be the best one in the country at that time, and she had just stumbled upon it. So, at least one of us benefited from Duke.

I had a year left on my contract and had a research grant that provided additional salary. This would give me time to complete some ongoing research and to apply for another academic position. Nevertheless, I felt humiliated and subconsciously needed to save face or, at least, not to show my face in the department that had rejected me. Without realizing this, I decided to grow a beard. The old, clean-shaven Paul disappeared, replaced by

The author at Northwestern University, 1974

a newly hirsute, more instinctual Paul—perhaps the hippie or the Samson-seeking Paul.

Part of that instinctual sense of self was to bring my social conscience into the classroom, and hopefully into some new research directions as well. Outside of the classroom at Duke, I had been very active in protesting the Vietnam War and later in keeping Richard Nixon from getting an honorary degree. Nixon had graduated from the Duke Law School near the top of his class. In a foreshadowing of Watergate, he had, as a student, engineered a break-in of the law school dean's office and had rifled through the files to see if his main rival for top honors had better grades. Our small group was successful in mobilizing the faculty and preventing Nixon from receiving the coveted honor.

I had earlier volunteered to teach a course called Psychology and International Relations. At the time, I thought I was being a good departmental citizen, but I learned later that my colleagues in experimental psychology viewed this as a frivolous use of my time. Many of them also felt the same way about the faculty protesting the war. The course was a huge success. Students actually loved the textbook, Jerome Frank's *Sanity & Survival: Psychological Aspects of War and Peace*, so much that many of them bought an extra copy to send home to their parents.

Based on this experience and my own concern for social issues, I decided to offer a new course called Psychological Approaches to Contemporary Social Problems. This was the era of Lyndon Johnson's Great Society, and there was a tremendous amount of activity addressing societal ills. New programs were being developed to deal with problems ranging from drug addiction to be handled in the new community mental health centers to remedial education using the Head Start preschool intervention. Students had to intern in a social service agency, develop an assessment of a service or intervention program, present it to the class in the presence of their internship supervisor, and submit the paper to him or her, as well as to me, for grading.

My major problem with this course was trying to apply psychological approaches to assess the effectiveness of these interventions. Then, one day, a famous social psychologist from Northwestern University came to campus to give a talk on just this topic. His name was Donald Campbell and his lecture was an epiphany. He had developed a systematic approach that used the experimental methods of psychology to evaluate what he called *ameliorative social programs*. I listened with increasing admiration and amazement as he described this methodology based on a set of quasi-experiments—that is, studies lacking random assignment of persons to a program group and a no-program control group—which he teasingly referred to as "queasy experiments." Here was my Moses presenting his commandments, or "threats to internal validity" (alternative explanations of the results), for finding the truth. They would guide me for the next thirty years until I retired.

As my job prospects for continuing an academic career in cognitive psychology dwindled with each rejection letter, fate intervened. Not only was I a convert to Campbell's approach to social problem solving, but also there was a job opening suitable for Camille at Northwestern starting in the fall of 1972. Although it was not Camille's first choice, Professor Campbell was also eager to hire, and even train, me to run his new postgraduate educational program in evaluation research. So, it was off to Evanston, Illinois (immediately north of Chicago). My wilderness years had ended.

Epilogue. To celebrate we purchased two brand new cars— a Toyota Corolla wagon and a Fiat 128 (later infamous as the Yugo)—both for a total of $5,000. The salesman was so thrilled with the dual commissions (which he claimed to need for his son who was a midget with a bone disease) that he personally hand-delivered a bonus surprise gift—a sixteen-ounce bag of prized Acapulco gold marijuana! And yes, I did inhale.

My Work: School Desegregation Research

We can recognize our prejudice and illusions only when, from a broader psychological knowledge of ourselves and others, we are prepared to doubt the absolute rightness of our assumptions and compare them carefully and conscientiously with the objective facts.

—C. G. Jung (2006, 100)

During my years in the Psychology Department at Northwestern University from 1972–79, I became first an apprentice to and then a colleague of Donald T. Campbell. Don, as he asked those with a PhD to call him, was a true modern, Renaissance scholar. He collaborated with anthropologists, philosophers, political scientists, sociologists, and statisticians on numerous research studies. Moreover, Don was a tireless and enthusiastic truth seeker who was constantly pushing the boundaries of the scientific method.

The heart of Campbell's approach was a systematic examination of the validity of the methods employed in social science research that he conducted with Julian Stanley and, later, with another colleague in psychology at Northwestern, Thomas Cook. The result was an elaborate and extensive set of so-called threats to validity which he called *plausible rival hypotheses*. Don was not satisfied in merely identifying problems with studies but in developing statistical adjustments for minimizing the biases that they introduced.

My interest in Don's approach was in extending it from a single study to an entire set of studies examining a single hypothesis such as the effect of coronary-artery bypass surgery on mortality. A new quantitative method called meta-analysis, which allowed one to combine data from multiple studies, had just appeared during this time. Meta-analysis required the random assignment of subjects to various conditions—the hallmark of a good study, or so-called true experiment, according to Campbell. Unfortunately, in all too many cases, the randomization process either was not done or was improperly implemented, resulting in a quasi-experiment.

At this time, a young sociology professor from the University of Chicago, Robert Crain, started coming up to Northwestern for advice on his work synthesizing the results of the quasi-experimental studies of school desegregation. Bob was a big fan of Campbell's, but he lacked the skills to apply those concepts to his own research. He then began a relentless, and ultimately, successful campaign to get me involved in conducting such a quantitative synthesis. While my interest lay in the area of health research, fate, in the form of a million-dollar grant from the U.S. National Institute of Education (NIE), intervened. It was not until the fall of 1979 when I left Northwestern with sufficient NIE research funds that I could commit to do this work. By that time, Crain had conducted and published his own study, but its methodology was both antiquated and flawed. He gladly agreed to send his entire data archive to me at the University of Michigan.

There I began a major collaborative effort with Fred Bryant, a postdoctoral fellow with whom I had previously worked when he was a doctoral student at Northwestern. We laboriously read all of Crain's collected studies while also searching out new ones from places as far away as Gulfport, Mississippi. I remember getting the last, coffee-stained, dog-eared, flyspecked copy of Gulfport's in-house evaluation of their district's desegregation. Over a year later, we had an elaborately coded and documented archive of all published and unpublished studies. After sifting through the data, eliminating fatally flawed studies, and adjusting for various biases, we found that one year of public school desegregation led to an average gain on standardized tests of reading and math achievement in African American students of two months—a socially significant as well as statistically significant educational benefit.

At that point, I was contacted by an official of the U. S. government and was asked to serve on a commission convened by President Ronald Reagan to examine the effects of school desegregation on achievement. The official was using what I called the Noah's Ark principle to compose the panel. There would be two researchers who were pro-desegregation, two against, and two who were neutral. My former colleague, Tom Cook, had agreed to be the methodological consultant. Since I had found results favoring desegregation, I was one of the "pro" members; Bob Crain was the other.

Once we all met in Washington, D.C., it became immediately clear that I had the only complete data set. All the others, with the exception of Crain, had conducted just one study. Most of these were so flawed that they were not usable in my final analysis. So the committee decided to have the other five panelists reanalyze my data. Crain soon opted out, standing by his initial synthesis based on a much smaller set of studies. Over the next year, I received endless daily calls from one or more of the panelists as they undertook their own analyses and watched in frustrated and irritated resignation as they substituted their own subjective and undocumented criteria for our rigorous, objective ones.

At the conclusion, we had six people with six different results that mirrored their own views of the benefits of desegregation. They ranged from the Crain's high, pro-desegregation result to archconservative David Armor's near zero, but still positive, finding. Nevertheless, everyone found a beneficial result for desegregation and the average was only slightly lower than the one that Fred Bryant and I had found. In light of this, Tom Cook suggested that the group issue a consensus statement to that effect. The conservative anti-desegregation members vetoed this idea, and the panel's convener then proceeded to prohibit our report from receiving a presidential seal. He also tried to have the final report embargoed from public dissemination.

Three events then occurred. First, one of the panelists—a supposedly neutral member—confessed to me that the panel was, in fact, rigged and that he and the other "neutral" member were actually against school desegregation! And so the dark face behind the conservative Howdy-Doody mask worn by Ronald Reagan was revealed. Ironically, I had just joined Michigan's Center for Research on the Utilization of Scientific Knowledge, and my first lesson was that political ideology would try to undermine the utilization of valid scientific results. The agenda was all about discrediting public school desegregation to appease Southern conservatives and, in so doing, allow tax funds to go via public school vouchers to private schools run by pro-business and anti–teachers union Republicans. It was an example of what Jung would call the "collective shadow"—those repressed, dark aspects of ourselves—projected onto others. In this case, the scapegoats were African American children.

Second, the results of the study, including this panel exercise, were published in a scientific journal (see Wortman and Bryant, 1985). Third and finally, Tom Cook decided to wage a personal campaign to have the report released. Using the Freedom of Information Act he finally succeeded in having the report made available to the public. With an accompanying press release, the report allowed the scientific validity of one small beacon of truth to shine. As Campbell (1991, 240) prophetically advocated in a landmark paper on social experimentation, "We need historical studies of corruption and influence attempts…where the record keeping has been both more corrupted and less." Jung (1991, 74) pointed to the shadow basis for such corruption when he observed, "There is a deep gulf between what a man is and what he represents, between what he is as an individual and what he is as a collective being."

My Work: The Consensus Development Program Evaluation

Man needs difficulties; they are necessary for health.

—C. G. Jung (1969e, 73)

During the spring, 1978 my wife's Northwestern University colleague, Philip Brickman, informed her that he'd be leaving that fall to become the director of the illustrious Research Center for Group Dynamics (RCGD) at the University of Michigan's Institute for Social Research (ISR). There was an additional position available in his center that he thought Camille could obtain. Thus began an ultimately successful campaign to convince me to relocate to Ann Arbor and accept an academic position at Michigan. While Evanston, Illinois, the home of Northwestern, may not have been Athens, as my first mentor, Herbert Simon, said about Pittsburgh, to me it certainly was Renaissance Florence with my new mentor, Donald Campbell, being Prince Medici.

By the fall of 1979, my wife and I had both been offered and accepted positions at Michigan, she in psychology and RCGD, and I in the School of Public Health and in ISR's Center for Research on the Utilization of Scientific Knowledge (CRUSK). Our academic appointments were for twelve months—split half time during the nine-month academic year and then full-time at ISR for the summer. Since ISR was funded entirely by the indirect costs the federal government paid research institutions (about 50 cents for every dollar of research expense), we were responsible for paying 62.5 percent of our annual salary. So the pressure to submit and obtain research grants was immediate and unrelenting.

I was successful with my very first project proposal—a large contract to evaluate an innovative program developed and run out of the nation's premier health research agency, the National Institutes of Health (NIH). Under pressure from both Senator Edward Kennedy and the Reagan administration, the NIH had created a Consensus Development (CD) Program to assess innovative medical technologies like coronary-artery bypass graft surgery and hip joint replacement and to disseminate their findings to the medical community as well as to the public.

The CD program consisted of a series of three-day conferences run like a trial, addressing a set of specific questions, such as safety and effectiveness, about the technology. A CD panel consisting of nationally renowned, but neutral, scholars heard two days of testimony from experts throughout the world on all relevant aspects of the technology and then adjourned on the evening of the second day to write a verdict or CD statement. The statement was read the next morning for comments by the audience, often composed of representatives from the medical industry, and routinely published in one of the nation's preeminent medical journals, the Journal of the American Medical Association.

The director of the CD program was a burly, balding, cigar smoking, and imposing physician named Charles Upton Lowe. Like most program directors, he wanted a favorable evaluation of his program, but unlike most, Charlie, we soon learned, would stop at nothing to make sure it happened. To my astonishment, Charlie rejected the first quarterly progress report we submitted that described the major CD program elements and our proposed evaluation plans even though we were careful to parrot back most of the information he had provided to us in describing the program's operation. He accused us of "rushing to judgment" and ordered us to rethink and revise the report. This was just the beginning of a series of intimidation attempts, which we, with a sense of gallows humor, called "Lowe blows," that Charlie was to dish out.

Things finally reached a crisis when Charlie and his doppelganger assistant, Itzhak (Itzy) Jacoby, suspended all work on the evaluation for six months while he tried to have my colleague, Lee Sechrest, whom I'd worked closely with at Northwestern and then brought in as the new CRUSK director, assume total control of the project. Lee even went so far as to take me out to lunch with that purpose in mind. Fortunately, Camille, whose political antennae were always more sensitive than mine, saw this planned coup coming and joined us, helping me fend off this attempted betrayal.

I felt beleaguered and tempted to terminate the project, but one of my famous ISR colleagues and collaborators told me, with straight-faced hyperbole, that it was a matter of honor to demonstrate the value of social science research in the face of conservative, Reaganite skeptics. I found more meaningful solace from the head of the Oversight Committee for the CD program evaluation, Henry Riecken. Hank was an eminent social psychologist, a coauthor of a major evaluation book with Donald Campbell, and a man of iron-willed principle who could stare down a bully like Charlie Lowe. With his support, I was able to move forward with the scientific work specified to complete the evaluation. It never dawned on me that I was up against anything more than a nasty, arrogant man who wanted desperately to look good by having the CD Program that he'd developed be given a seal of approval.

Then, one day, I began a phase of the evaluation that required me to interview the chairs of previous CD panels. The first man I called seemed to have been waiting for that moment. To my amazement, he claimed that Dr. Lowe had committed fraud by personally altering the consensus statement written by his panel. Although we had witnessed Charlie badger and bully an MIT professor over some technical language in a draft

CD statement until, in exasperation, the man relented, saying, "I'll delete the paragraph if you'll delete your cigar." However, this accusation was beyond anything I imagined. It required corroboration that was soon forthcoming from other members of that panel. I felt that we had no choice but to include this in our final report. And we did.

Epilogue. Before I could even hand it to him, Itzy grabbed the copy of our two-hundred-plus page final report containing our findings and recommendations from my hands, and we were summarily dismissed. There would be no eighteen-month follow-up experiment as originally promised. We learned a few months later that, as a consequence of our findings, Charlie Lowe had been fired as director, with Itzy taking over. Charlie, we were told, had been relegated to handling patents with no staff or supervisory functions in a small windowless office. A few years later, I read of a private plane that had crashed in northern New Jersey, killing all on board. The pilot was identified as Itzhak Jacoby.

Phil Brickman, who had brought Camille and me to Michigan, did not fare any better. His 1960s-style "participatory democracy" approach to governing RCGD was strongly resisted and disliked by his more patriarchal, authoritarian colleagues. He was institutionalized in a psychiatric hospital and, upon his release, during the time of this project, jumped to his death from the top of the twenty-two-story Bell Tower Plaza, just around the corner from ISR.

Within a year of completing the CD evaluation, Lee Sechrest asked to meet with Camille and me in my ISR office. He informed us that he was leaving to become chair of the psychology department at the University of Arizona in Tucson. In an act of contrition, he invited us to join him as full professors. Before I could take it all in and say yes, Camille replied, "Thanks, Lee. That's really very nice of you, but at this time, we're not ready to move." I was flabbergasted as I, too, wanted to leave

Ann Arbor with its interminable, bitter-cold, gray, sunless winters and equally frosty, power-obsessed faculty.

It took me over two years to work through all the emotional scars left by the CD evaluation and to write a coherent scientific paper about it. The article was immediately accepted by one of the two coeditors of the major journal in the field, *The International Journal of Technology Assessment in Health Care.* A few months later, however, I was asked to meet with the other coeditor, a Swedish researcher, while attending a conference in Washington, D.C. He informed me that he was withdrawing the acceptance of the paper. He felt the CD program, which had been adopted by many European countries including Sweden, should be protected from criticism. It was the final Lowe blow in this thoroughly toxic episode that would ironically be the last program evaluation I ever conducted.

Luck then finally smiled on me. My colleague at The University of Michigan's School of Public Health, Larry Brown, happened to be editor of the *Journal of Health Politics, Policy and Law.* He immediately accepted the paper for publication (see Wortman, Vinokur, and Sechrest 1988).

The New Year: Farewell to the First Half of Life

The afternoon of human life must also have significance of its own and cannot be merely a pitiful appendage to life's morning.

—C. G. Jung (1969c, 399)

Just before Christmas 2008, the chair of the psychology department informed me that I would have to give up the office I'd kept since retiring in 2001. A week into the New Year I took an empty box and filled it with the few remaining items of significance. The following poem, first composed in 2004, has been revised to express what I discovered as I completed this task.

Emptying My Office and Finding What I Lost

How long was it
since my e-mail to you
disappeared into
some dead-letter
emptiness?
Was it a year ago? Two?
The last time we met
at Starbucks for
cappuccino,
you were now transformed
from a student chrysalis
into a glittering young
woman
gushing your professional
dreams.

Then in the parking lot,
your face burst open
the night; your blonde hair
spiraled out in tangles
of solar flares
that engulfed me
into the vortex
of your embrace
in a brief good-bye.

Now, seven years later
I'm emptying my office
of all those things
that seemed so essential.
And there guarding

the barren shelves
a photo beckons—
your graduation—
you, the star student,
my honors advisee,
class valedictorian.

Your spiritual mentor,
Sister Margaret sent it.
She'd asked me what
I admired most in you.

"Her big heart," I said,
and she wept.

Perhaps there was more
that I could teach,
but you gave more
than I could hope—
a hug, our two smiles
lighting the universe
and forever validating
34 years of teaching.

Graduation, 1999: The author with Carmelina Lalley

4 Loss

My Year of Death: Mother

Dreaming back thru life, Your time—and mine accelerating toward Apocalypse, the final moment
                    —Alan Ginsberg, "Kaddish"

Death is that inevitable duality to life. We all know it. But knowing it and feeling it, I discovered are two separate issues. By that I don't mean just grief and loss, although they certainly are part of our meeting with death. It is the ultimate question that the trivial burdens of life try so conveniently to distract us from, the question we all must eventually confront: "What does it mean?"

In 1998, I entered my year of death. In case I was not paying attention, death visited me three times in eight months, each time claiming a younger victim. Death, of course, has no more respect for age than it does calendars, and my death year began on December 23, 1997. That was the beginning of Chanukah and the day my mother died at age eighty-five after a long descent into Alzheimer's disease. It seemed to be the disease of choice in her family, having earlier claimed her mother and more recently the youngest of her three sisters.

My feelings about my mother were ambivalent at best. Just a few years earlier, I had a "recovered memory" of a very disturbing traumatic event. When I was age four, my mother had rubbed a dirty diaper in my face (see chapter 5, Sh*t Happens!). Unlike other recovered memories, I knew this one was real. It came almost unbidden after being submerged in my unconscious for fifty years. There was no pressure to shape it on my part or my therapist's. It also was so unusual that it defied the common stereotype of sexual abuse. It was just old-fashioned abuse, if somewhat unusual in form. Moreover, I had both extremely strong cognitive and affective reactions to this recovered memory.

On the cognitive or intellectual side, the memory was immediately fresh, vivid, and all too real after resting in its hiding place for decades. At fifty-five, I knew it wasn't a "senior moment" but was the truth. If that weren't proof enough, my emotional reaction was, as the research literature confirmed, overwhelmingly powerful. I was so stunned that I could literally barely move. My therapist proved of little help as I heard him murmur, "Oh my God." (He later denied having uttered the phrase and did not pursue it except to make "shit in your face" jokes.) Our session ended, I stumbled out of his office into the beautiful sunny warmth of spring and then somehow managed to drive home despite the intense trembling coursing through me.

This memory was consistent with many others involving constant criticism that left scars of enduring inadequacy. Fortunately, they never completely overwhelmed me. My mother was my protector from my father, but the price was very high. I was her servant and errand boy—her Cinderfella. I remember how I would go from store to store to do her weekend shopping and how, at each place, the clerk would inform me that my mother had just called with additional requests. Then, when I returned, she would, with uncanny and unerring radar, immediately notice the one item I had forgotten to purchase and would berate me for the omission. To this day, I cannot shop for groceries without missing one item on the list. Camille and I jokingly call it the Julia Wortman effect.

Praise was also something my mother reserved largely to enhance her own self-esteem. When she entertained her women friends, I would often overhear her boasting about my accomplishments. She would never praise me directly or empower me with it. It was only to demonstrate to others that she was the Good Mother.

In another early memory, I recall opening the bottom drawer of my mother's dresser and being totally astonished by the dozens of beautiful pencil drawings I discovered of scenes and persons. There was an entire artistic side to my mother that I had never seen. In 1972, when she finally left my father after thirty-six strife-filled years of marriage, that side of her magically reappeared. She took up oil painting and produced series of marvelous canvasses.

My mother also began dating, which I, as a recently married man, found amusing. I remember her complaining about her seventy-four-year-old boyfriend. "Men! They only want one thing." And this man had insisted on having it a minimum of three times per week. Fortunately, my mother soon met Harold Zwerdling. He was infinitely kind, patient, and loving. He was totally devoted to her. And, she happily reported, he was impotent.

During this time, there were some significant healing moments. My mother finally had the good sense to tell Camille and me that she was sorry for having initially opposed our marriage—a phone conversation that Camille had inadvertently overheard. She realized that Camille had made me happy and had finally told her so.

Jung tells us that life really is the conflict or "tension of opposites," and my mother certainly represented that to me.

While I might not forgive her for what my clueless therapist had jokingly referred to as my "shit in the face" experience, I could, after considerable inner work, take back my anger and choose to remember the good times. I had been on healing journeys to Greece and decided to write a final poem to my mother's memory stocked with only positive recollections of some of the nice places she had taken me. It would honor the good Julia and bury the bad. However, my older brother, Alan, still needing to exert control, kept me from reading the poem at the gravesite. Fortunately, my mother's sisters objected and insisted that I read the following poem aloud at the reception that followed. And, to his credit, Alan openly praised the poem.

Mother: In Memoriam*

The sun has set; where are my sons?
    Now, light the first candle!
It will remove the eternal shroud of darkness.
    Pray that they will find me
(savoring a meal at the Far East Garden or
at the Spaghetti Palace).

"Blessed are You, the Force that rules
    all of existence,
Who sanctifies us by giving us a way
    of life directed by holy commandments
and commanded us to light
    the lights of Chanukah."

Eight awesome days the light flickered.
    Let us celebrate the Maccabee's victory.
Eight amazing decades my life glowed.
    Pray that my spirit will be free
(laughing at Dutchland Farms or Riverside Park).

"Blessed are You, the Force that rules
    the universe,
Who made possible miracles
    for our ancestors, in those days,
and also makes the same possible
    for us in our own time."

Eight splendid men have been the gifts
    of my life:
sons—Alan, Paul, and Ron;
    Grandsons—
Joshua and Jed, Jeremy and Andrew;
    and my steadfast, glowing companion—Harold.

Pray that they still see me
(grinning in the dark of the Allyn or Strand theater).

Blessed are You, the Force that rules
      the family of all men and women,
Who shines upon us through the ages
      and allows us to bear the fruit
that renews one generation with another.

Eight mortal spirits have illuminated
      your lives:
my parents—Fannie and Robert;
your aunts and uncles—
Jack and Jeanette, Ida and Izzie;
      your father—Max, and now
me, your mother—Julia.
      Pray that my soul will shine
(smiling on the waters of Barkhamsted or Ocean
      Beach).

Blessed are You, the Force that rules
      the day and the night,
Who has kept us in life—
      and in death,
and made it possible
      for us to join together now
(and at all the happy places we have been)!

Amen.

*Quoted material from *Tikkun*, vol. 12, November/December, 1997.

My Year of Death: Alan

beyond any blessing and song,
praise and consolation that are uttered in the world
—**Mourner's Kaddish**

In early January 1998, my family gathered for the burial of my mother. She had wanted to be cremated, and I had some romantic *Bridges of Madison County* vision that we'd then spread her ashes in some beautiful place. My older brother, Alan, who was very religious, informed me that according to Judaic custom her remains still had to be buried. The only cemetery plot available was beside my father, whom she'd divorced over twenty years earlier and, I was quite sure, whom she had no intention of rejoining for eternity. I was able to arrange for a swap of plots that placed my mother one row away.

Jung (1969b, 409-410) tells us "to regard death as the fulfillment of life's meaning and its goal in the truest sense, instead of a mere meaningless cessation." This might be true for me personally, but for Alan it was not. Just two weeks after my mother's burial, I received a call from him at my office. He informed me tearfully that he'd just been diagnosed with pancreatic cancer. I knew from my own medical research on prostate cancer that it is one of the most deadly of all organ cancers with a life expectancy of only five months. When I checked the NIH Web site, I realized that my brother's cancer had probably metastasized. Alan seemed aware of the prognosis when he obliquely mentioned the research literature. Nevertheless, he decided to have surgery performed locally, noting that one could live with only one-third of their pancreas.

Ever since Governor Pataki had put a temporary stop to New York state employee dental benefits in 1996, I had been driving up to Alan's dental office in Southington, Connecticut, for treatment. We'd have lunch together and do some long-neglected bonding to catch up on the years I'd lived so far away. I had hoped that our two families would spend more time together, but that just never happened. By 1997, Alan was planning to sell his practice and move to Arizona the following year where he'd be just a part-time dentist. After his surgery in February, he told me he was feeling too ill to finish my dental work. Instead, I accompanied him to his haircut appointment and then to his home for a visit. Despite some residual surgical pain, he seemed stoically optimistic about his health, the final sale of his practice, and the planned move to Tucson.

Two months later, I was teaching when my sister-in-law called my wife to tell her that Alan had been hospitalized and his situation was grave. By the time I got home Camille had packed our bags and we set off for Hartford Hospital on the Port Jefferson ferry. It was a grim, gray night with fog-shrouded fine mist enveloping the ferry and angry, dark, foam-crowned waves tossing the boat. Like Odysseus, I felt as if I was in the company of Charon crossing the River Styx into Hades. We arrived at the hospital one hour after reaching Bridgeport. It was just seven minutes after my brother had passed away at age sixty-one.

I entered Alan's hospital room and knelt at the edge of his bed. I let out a scream that became a wail and finally a quiet moan. I said a short prayer and then inexplicably ran my hand through his curly gray-blond hair in a gesture of farewell. My sister-in-law and her family then accompanied me as we all left the hospital into the dreary night.

The suddenness of Alan's death sent both his wife and me into an emotional shock. Fortunately, Camille stepped in to provide the immediate care we needed. She drafted the obituary and met with the funeral director to negotiate a much fairer, and significantly lower, cost. With Camille's help, I managed to write a little poem that I was somehow able to read at the grave after placing a shovelful of dirt on his coffin. The poem that follows briefly recounted his many achievements as a talented amateur sculptor, masters-level bridge player, champion dancer, and member of his synagogue's choir.

To Alan: A Farewell Remembrance

I have dreams dear Alan—of you
     singing, dancing, sculpting, writing.
I have memories dear Alan—of you
     son, brother, father, husband.

First-born son of Julia and Max
     singing of God's glory in the all-city choir.
On this day when God called forth the first born
     and set His people free,
He called you to join His chorus
     and set you free from the burden of mortality.

Elder brother of Paul and Ron
     dancing a fox trot to life's rhythms
and winning the school championship.
     You held our hand at the start of life's dance
and showed us how to take the first steps.
     Now we hold you in our hands as the music
fades
and we dance our last steps together.

Father of Joshua and Jed
     sculpting a life together
showing them that dreams are chipped away
     only to reveal art in life and
giving them the courage
     to sculpt life in art.

Husband to Susan Spanier
     writing many chapters of life's voyages
stories of adventures
     in France, Greece, and Israel
that we could only dream of.

You knew dear Alan
    that dreams alone are life's work.
You looked death in the eye
    and dared to dream
And where your dreams end
    our memories begin.
May you rest forever in the embrace
    of the nurturant love and creative vision
    you bequeathed us all.
Sweet dreams dear Alan.

I really wasn't able to get fully in touch with my emotions for over a year. At that point, I wrote the following poem, "The Paper Bag," which was published a few years later (Wortman 2004). It describes one of those little details at the time of death that become indelible and come to take on a larger, symbolic meaning, as is often the case in poetry. The poem gestated in me during that time, and like the traditional unveiling of the gravestone, it represents the final farewell that I did not get to say to Alan at that terrible moment.

The Paper Bag

It was a plain, brown
paper bag
just like the ones in
the supermarket,
filled with items
to sustain us
that the clerk hands you with
a canned smile
and a prerecorded admonition to
" have a nice day."

I first saw it when
I came to visit you.
Your wife was cradling it
gently
just like a newborn.
We didn't glance back,
but walked together in quiet
communion
through the hospital's
maze
emerging in darkness
shrouded
with a tearful mist.

I saw it the next day when
I went to your home
standing mutely in the hallway
alone in the shadows
just like some night watchman
guarding your sculptures—
time-worn monuments to
your past.

It was still there
a few days later
when we stopped by to bid
you good-bye
just like some mournful
ghost
that no one wanted to
recognize.

There it beckoned to me
one last time
and I wistfully inventoried
its contents
just like items for a final
clearance—
shoes on top,
pants in the middle,
shirt on the bottom—
a life stood on its head and
emptied out.

My Year of Death: Meghan

Death is a fearful thing. ...
I am so out of love
with life that I will sue to be rid of it.

—William Shakespeare, Measure for Measure

After Alan's death, I returned to my professorial duties, hoping for some useful distraction. The distractions of the school year ended faster than I wanted, and the summer brought Meghan further into our lives. She was a brilliant, but troubled, undergraduate who'd been outstanding in my research methods class. I had then asked her to be one of my three undergraduate teaching assistants the following semester. It was during that time that she sought my advice in fleeing an abusive relationship. As she tearfully confided in me, I noticed the faint scars on her tanned arms and realized that she had been cutting herself. Always a rescuer at heart (Jung would say I had too much of the martyr/rescuer archetype), I got her a position working for Camille, who needed extra help and had the resources to pay for it.

During the summer, Meghan began working in my wife's basement office. As the months wore on, her mood darkened. She claimed that her depression was due to some recent medical problems indicating that she might never be able to have children. Her downward spiral continued as she learned that the prognosis was not good. One Monday in late August, she did not show up for work. Camille was concerned given Meghan's situation. I, too, had a gut feeling that something was not right. Since Camille was then away on a business trip, she asked if I'd be willing to drive over to Port Jefferson to check on Meghan.

I arrived at the house where Meghan rented a second-floor room and saw her car parked in front. At that moment, my heart sank in fear. When no one answered her bell, I went up and knocked on her door. Again, there was no response. As I was about to leave, I encountered one of her downstairs neighbors. I told her my concerns, and she said we could climb out a low window onto the flat roof and look in to Meghan's room. I followed her back up the stairs and stepped out the window and onto the roof. We approached Meghan's window and peered in. The nightmarish fears we all have were realized in that moment. I saw Meghan lying on her bed with a bag over her head. We called the police, who forced open the locked door and confirmed that Meghan had, indeed, committed suicide over the weekend. She was just twenty-two years old.

This third death in a span of eight months was more than I could cope with. Fortunately, I had a friend, Ed Tick, who was a therapist specializing in healing from such traumatic events and with whom, with Jungian like synchronicity, I had already planned to visit later that very week. My wife and I arrived at his home in Albany, New York, in late August for a special ceremony, a *glendi*, he had arranged that would follow ancient Greek practices. We read some poems by Pindar together, and, following the Greek tradition, we offered a toast to Meghan's departed soul so that she might have a good crossing to the other world.

At the conclusion of this memorial service, Ed invited me to accompany him on a healing trip he'd organized to Greece and Turkey that October. He was planning to visit a number of ancient sites dedicated to the Greek god Asklepios. The followers of Asklepios included Galen and Hippocrates, who established a network of over six hundred hospitals, or *asklepia*, offering cures for both physical and mental health problems. Upon my return home, I wrote to Ed, saying, "I think I may need, for my own sake, to make this pilgrimage with you. I feel like Job—my faith is sorely tested. Death is at my elbow, and each blow becomes more severe and more tragic."

We left New York on Columbus Day for Athens and then, after a short taxi ride to its port city, Piraeus, would go by boat to the island of Poros. On the plane, I noted, "This is an inner journey—a flight to the soul, to healing." On Poros, we visited many sites sacred to both the ancients and moderns. As we entered a beautiful old monastery, I felt the departed voices call out to me and wrote the following poem.

At the Monastery

Through heaven's half-open door
    your spirits caress me.
It is healed and healing.
    The illness of life
has released you—
    no longer crucified, but
whole and holy.
    I bless, am blessed,
forgive, am forgiven.
    The tears cleanse and
are wiped away
    by the whisper of your
immortal psyches.

This was followed a few days later by a healing vision at Epidauros. Little remains of what was the largest healing site in the ancient world, known for its magnificent theater where today the plays of the ancient Greeks are performed. After exploring the entire site, I returned to the ruins near the amphitheater. I sat under a tree at the far end from the entrance perched on an ancient wall. I closed my eyes to concentrate and meditate. A strange vision appeared of billowing, cloudlike foam. It bubbled up until it covered everything. Then, almost immediately, clear cleansing water started to dissolve the foam. The water continued to flow and spread until all the opaque foam had been washed away. I opened my eyes and everything seemed clearer and more vibrant. My friend and guide told me afterward that the spot where I had this vision was the site of the Temple to Asklepios.

My healing continued throughout the two-week trip culminating in an important dream the night before we visited the ancient, but still intact, dream chambers of the asklepion in

Pergamum, now Bergama, in Turkey. In that dream, I yelled, "No more death!" as I went to the aid of a colleague who had callously wounded me (see the prologue).

As Jung (1989, 314) wrote, "[D]eath is indeed a fearful piece of brutality;...not only as a physical event, but far more so psychically". So it was for me. Upon my return home, I realized that it was time to let my academic career die as well. I entered into negotiations with the dean and officially retired from Stony Brook University at the end of 2001. I was sixty-one and one-half years old—the same age as my brother, Alan, when he died.

Max

And you, my father, there on the sad height,
Curse, bless, me now with your fierce tears, I pray.

—Dylan Thomas, "Do Not Go Gentle into that
Good Night"

I'm looking at the weekly King Kullen grocery ad and noticing all the specials for Passover food. Passover starts a week from today, and for me, it is truly a time to commemorate the tenth plague—the death of the firstborn. My father, Max, the eldest of Lena's five children, passed away on this holiday seventeen years ago. And ten years ago, my brother, Alan, the firstborn of Max's children, had died, also during Passover. As I look at the foods for sale, I see the borscht, the herring, the kippers, and gefilte fish that Max savored. Those were the only things that he seemed to enjoy other than the Sunday evening *Ed Solomon Show* (it may have been "Ed Sullivan" to you, but he was an honorary member of the Jewish tribe according to Max).

How could it be otherwise for a son of The Bubby, who had firm control over his development while her husband, the patriarchal Abraham, left them to find his way to and in the New World. Abraham first became a street peddler of fruits and vegetables, then a very successful businessman with his grocery store, A. Wortman & Sons. He died suddenly of a heart attack in his early fifties just two months before Alan was born and named for him. The rage Max must have felt at losing his father during his formative years as a new husband and father—and at his overbearing, neurotic mother—spilled over constantly into our family, especially onto my mother and her mama's boy, a second-born, me. Of course, my mother, Julia, was herself the granddaughter of Little Bubby, who supposedly had ten husbands (see I Remember Fanny in chapter 1). Little Bubby clearly had been hard on men as was her daughter (my grandmother), Fanny, and now my mother. They all relished dominating weak men.

And so it was that I grew up on this battlefield. The trauma was exacerbated by Max's seemingly constant attempts to chase me down with a kitchen knife in hand whenever he was angry with me. Of course, he never really caught me, but once when I was seven, I slipped as I was diving for a secure hiding place under my bed. As I fell, my new front tooth caught the edge of the bed and was cleanly knocked out. It was a weekend, and we didn't know you could save the tooth. Consequently, I was saddled with wearing very unsightly gold braces to hold in a false tooth that were a constant source of embarrassing questions and a disturbing reminder of my father's angry legacy. Not until twenty years later was I finally able to get proper dental care.

Six days a week Max would leave for work at 5 a.m. and not return until between 9 and 10 that evening after stopping off to see The Bubby and having a drink or two. Even on Sundays he would often sneak away to open up for half a day in clear violation of the "blue laws." My few attempts to get close to Max by working for him were all failures. He didn't like the way I swept the grocery store, so he fired me. I was a math whiz so he asked me to keep the books, but that job was removed as well. Years later, Alan reminded me of that event and asked me, "Do you know why Max stopped letting you keep the books?"

"I've always wondered about that. What was the reason?" I asked.

"You always paid the bills on time, and Max never paid anyone until they threatened him."

When I was in high school, I had an auto accident and called home for help. Max screamed angrily through the phone; he was only concerned about the dent in the front bumper. So like the Biblical Abraham, I, too, made an exodus from Max, fleeing to my own new world of college, marriage, and finally, an academic career far from my childhood home. Although I attended Yale, only thirty miles from home, Max never once visited me. He didn't approve of my marriage to a goy and very reluctantly attended the wedding, where he publicly insulted me by denigrating the value of my PhD.

Afterward, whenever I visited Alan at his home in West Hartford, he would have Max there for Sunday brunch. Even then, I could never connect. He would project the usual guilt ("Why don't you ever call?") but refuse to engage in conversation. Max would talk at me, endlessly repeating all the same old stories (or *bobemayse*, as my mother called them in Yiddish), but never talk to me.

Then in 1991, the year after I'd relocated to nearby Long Island, Max was hospitalized for what turned out to be congestive heart failure. His doctor claimed he would soon be released and then left for the Passover holiday. Alan called to tell me that Max had passed away suddenly. We both felt intense rage at the physician for depriving us of one last attempt to reconcile with Max. We thought of writing a scathing letter, but Alan held back because the doctor's wife was an old and dear friend from his high school days who was currently his dental patient.

I was left to say my own good-bye. This is the farewell poem I read at Max's funeral on Passover/Easter Sunday, March 31, 1991.

Dad: In Memoriam

I have known the harsh lash
  of your mortality—
the angry pain of your presence,
and bear the verbal crucifix
  of your insecurity.

I have wandered in the wilderness
  of your silence—
the loneliness of your absence,
and followed you down the quiet,
   dark empty streets of existence.

I have sailed across the sea of knowledge.
I have walked through the valley of fear.
And, I have climbed the mountain of hope.

I have come at last to receive
   the words of the sacred covenant
   between Father and son.
I have come to plant the withered seed
  of your immortality.
And, I pray that it will finally blossom
  in the warm light of eternity.

On this day of release and redemption
I bear witness to your freedom
  from earthly bondage.
Now I can forgive the cruelty
  of winter,
and utter the holy words of spring:
   "acceptance," "love," and "rebirth."

Epilogue. One particular item in the King Kullen ad caught my attention---memorial or *yahrzeit* candles. For me Passover now had a truly archetypal meaning—the freedom from a father-Pharaoh figure and the spiritual journey it had foretold. I had long ago adopted the anti-Father approach to parenting, or as Jung would say (1968, 90), "Anything, so long as it is not like Father!" Where Max was absent; I was present. Where Max was hostile; I was gentle. Where Max was critical; I was supportive. Nevertheless, writing this memoir represented a major step toward closure.

To celebrate the spiritual aspect and finally to commemorate both Max's and Alan's passing, I purchased two candles. I then prepared a mini-Seder that focused on lighting the candles with the Passover blessing. A blessing of the matzo followed, and we concluded with eating the matzo along with the bitter herbs dipped in salt water. At sundown, I conducted the Seder with Camille and Andrew in attendance. We all shared the matzo, and then I opened a bottle of *prosecco*—an effervescent, white Italian wine—and offered the traditional toast, "*L'chaim* and best wishes for a good *Pesach*."

5 Complexes

Facing the Father-Complex

Why does the eye see a thing more clearly in dreams than the imagination when awake?

—Leonardo da Vinci (2008)

I am on the edge of a harbor called the Shatt-al-Arab. The water flows calmly in on one side and exits with force and turbulence on the other far (or right) side as one faces it. There has been an accident or tragedy. Some family members are standing there trying to find out what has happened to their loved ones who have either been kidnapped or swept out of the harbor. One has managed to return. It may be the father. The others are still missing. They appear to be Arabs. I approach them and offer my sincerest consolations, and put my hand on the shoulders of one of them, perhaps the father, and say, "I will be there for you." I offer to take up a collection to assist them with their needs and then leave, walking purposely and forcefully across a road-bridge over the water, which flows underneath. There's an observation tower on the right side of the harbor where it's possible to get a better view of the situation. I'm walking—ramrod straight with quick steps, almost robot like—and wearing an unusual hooded robe that is composed of long, offset rectangles colored in alternating browns and light greens somewhat like military camouflage clothing. The hood and sleeves have a two-inch black cloth border. I enter the tower and briskly start ascending the stairs. At a landing where there are elevators, my passage is barred by a small chain. There are other people there. A woman tells me that she has written instructions, which she shows me. She says that we can go around the chain to another bank of elevators. We all enter an elevator and the woman instructs me to press 3A (I think). The button is high up on the back and I'm the only one who can reach it. I press it repeatedly and do not think anything is happening. There's another button, but before I can push it, the woman yells not to touch it since it's the emergency and will stop everything. We then ascend very rapidly. Interestingly, instead of ascending straight up as in normal elevators, we are zigzagging up as if we were on stairs. I then recognize another woman in the elevator, but can't remember whom.

It was at this point that I actually woke up. Just like me to have a weird dream when I'm taking a class in Jungian dream analysis. But what the hell does it mean? I'm usually pretty good at this but don't have a clue what my unconscious is trying to tell me. At least, it doesn't seem to be about my anima issue (see the following and chapter 8), so maybe I can bring it into class and the instructor will decide to use it. Why not? I'm sixty-five for Christ's sake; time to go for it!

So, the instructor, a Jungian therapist, says to the class while turning to me, "Let's look at this dream. What associations do you have?" he asks me.

"Well, at first nothing came to mind," I said. "But then a couple of things. The Shatt-al-Arab was the place of intense conflict during the Iran–Iraq war where tens of thousands died. Then, the harbor, to me, was a heart pumping. And I know from our prior discussion that going up is going into one's head, but I also know that the robe of camouflage colors is the earth. So it appears that I'm also a bit grounded here. And the elevator taking a zigzag path like stairs reminds me of Yeats' poems 'The Winding Stair,' which are supposed to be and are very feminine."

"Okay," he says. "You're in a place of conflict. That's the 'exposition' or 'setting.' And, it seems quite serious as your heart is in it and could be wounded. Do you have any conflict in your life right now?"

"Well, as a matter of fact, I do. I'm in a retirement group that's in conflict with the dean who controls our organization."

"Do you usually get involved and take a leadership role in such conflicts?"

"Actually, it's not something I'd normally do, but, if I'm put in a position where it's required, I will respond. In fact, I met my wife at a Vietnam protest rally."

"Well, we have a father mentioned. How do you get along with your father?"

"He's been dead for fifteen years, but it was never good. I remember the day I got married and he reluctantly came to the wedding since my wife's not Jewish. It was the day after I got my PhD in psychology, and he said, 'Five years, and you're still not a real doctor.' In many Jewish homes then, there was tremendous pressure to be a professional like a physician or a lawyer."

"So then, how do you relate to your children?"

"I have two sons. My older son is just like his mother—straight A's in college, Phi Beta Kappa, marrying young. We get along well. And, interestingly, he's getting ready to apply to medical school! My younger son is much more like me—an artistic, sensitive, second-born who has to struggle a lot harder to succeed. This year has been a big turning point for both him and me. He never had that much good to say about me, but now it couldn't be better. We really seem to have come together."

"Let's just review the situation then. You're in a place of immense conflict. And you are in a conflict that's repeated between the dean and earlier your own father. We call that the father-complex. But then for the development of the plot part, you cross over the water to an elevator to get a better view or perspective on the conflict. What about the women you meet in the elevator, do you have any associations to them?"

"Not really."

"Then it appears that the "peripeteia," or the 'culmination of your crisis,' is about seeking resolution of your father-complex or conflict. You're in this priestly robe with a hood and going up. We call that, for a mature person your age, a 'head phallus.' You're reclaiming your phallic, or masculine energy, from your father. And you're doing that by getting in touch with your feminine, or compassionate, anima side; you're being guided by a woman and taking a feminine path to a solution. By the way, do you know what 3A is?"

"No, I don't."

"Well, I guess, despite your dream, you don't take the elevator up here or you'd know this is Room 3A. That's the only place it's posted."

Then, the *lysis*, or "unfolding after the crisis"—the "conclusion" or "solution"—hit me like the final piece of some gigantic, psychic jigsaw puzzle clicking into place. I had been battling an endless number of father figures culminating with the dean. The dream was not only about how to cope with the current struggle (its "orient" or moral imperative for action), but, more significantly, it cast light on the shadow, the negative father-complex that had plagued my entire conscious and unconscious adult life. I immediately decided to act by resigning my committee chairmanship, thereby terminating my involvement with the dean. On the train ride home from class, the following poem emerged to commemorate this moment and capture my feelings.

Facing My Father

What remains?
Some boozy smile,
a guilt-edged memory
to the tenderness
of pain.

A child's innocence
drowning in
the rejecting embrace—
a tsunami of words
scours away hope
leaving our shared burdens.

I was terrorized,
fleeing from
some inner demon—
stalking me
through the night,
through the day.

Months, years
then turning
looking at him
unafraid
giving back
the fear
asking for
my manhood.

So it was
a past
a wound

suffering
to tire Buddha
that taught
enlightenment
and love.

Sh*t Happens!

For what I feared has overtaken me,
What I dreaded has come upon me.

—Job 3:25

In his autobiography, *Memories, Dreams, Reflections*, Carl Jung (1989) describes an early, haunting childhood memory that tormented him over the next few days until he could confront it in its entirety (see Jung, 1989, 36-40). As he was walking home from school on one of those memorable radiant sunny days, he passed the cathedral and thought, "God made all this and sits above it far away in the blue sky on a golden throne..." He could not continue with this image since he felt "Something terrible is coming, something I do not want to think, something I dare not even approach." Jung struggled with this emerging thought over the next three nights until he found comfort in the realization that God had created the serpent to "induce Adam and Eve to sin." Taking this as a sign that "God also desires me to show courage," he then let his thoughts continue. This is what he envisioned. "God sits on His golden throne high above the world—and from under the throne an enormous turd falls upon the sparkling new roof, shatters it, and breaks the walls of the cathedral asunder."

So, what did young Carl Jung at age twelve make of this startling revelation that "sh*t happens"? He reports feeling "an unutterable bliss" at this profound insight into the "will of God" and, with it, "the miracle of grace which heals all and makes all comprehensible." But why, he thought, would "God befoul His cathedral?" At this point, he reports, "came the dim understanding that God could be something terrible." According to Jung, this was a turning point in his life. He says, "I had experienced a dark and terrible secret. It overshadowed my whole life, and I became pensive."

Like Jung, I, too, have struggled with some dark, disturbing memories from my childhood and wondered for many years if there was some missing explanation for them. I have carried the burden of these memories around like some haunted house that I can never move out of. Why did I kill that cat at age five? I love cats, still do. But I still remember wanting its affection and only receiving painful scratches. Oh, the rage and anger from my rejection. Why had I pushed my younger brother through the glass storm windows stored in our basement, giving him stitches and a scar? I knew this was not who I was and who I am. It was like some Jungian shadow figure, a Mr. Hyde, stalking the night of my childhood. I didn't seek forgiveness, just an explanation that would lighten my burden.

Fifty years went by with the memories, the guilt, and the remorse all intact. I packed these memories away, but they accompanied me as I moved from place to place like some steamer trunk from my youth. I knew the anger and neglect of my parents, but that they did not seem enough to explain my feelings. Something nagged at me; something was still hidden, something awful that I did not know or could not remember.

Jung, like Freud, had talked about and even demonstrated the existence of repression. Jung (1969a, 133) had said, "[T]he unconscious is the receptacle of all lost memories... [which] include all more or less intentional repressions of painful thoughts and feelings." Nevertheless, the concept of repressed memory is still controversial. It is nearly impossible to demonstrate scientifically, and many claim that such early memories are so easily manipulated by others, such as therapists, as to be unreliable. The wave of abusive memories that made headlines during the 1980s had even produced an opposition group called the False Memory Society of those parents who felt wrongly accused by their children.

All of this was of purely academic interest to me, as a psychologist teaching research methods, until I arrived at Stony Brook University. The transition was not an easy one for my family, especially my wife. As if her professional home as head of a new area in psychology was not dilapidated enough, the house we had built was a disaster as well (see Chapter 9, My House Is Not a Home). This threw her, a normally strong, stable woman, into a tailspin that only a psychotherapeutic intervention was able to correct. As part of the process, I also reluctantly agreed to enter therapy. And then, like Jung, I had my own cathartic cathedral experience, described in the following prose poem.

Recovered Memory

It came suddenly out of the grave of the past—the memory,
the shit!

I was sitting there—stunned—on the therapist's couch 50
years later

like some archaeologist digging up an awful truth.

Who would have thought that such an innocent question,

"Tell me a little about your mother?" would unearth such a
mummy's curse.

I was four; I wanted my mother's attention. But,

she was overwhelmed—three boys in seven years; a failing
marriage;

and now more diapers to change. Oh, she warned me, "Get
out of here!"

But I was four, and I needed her protection, and I wanted
her love.

Then my own Pearl Harbor struck as the bomb of a soiled
diaper

exploded onto my face and I ran in mortal pain from the
room

screaming, "I'll never forgive; I'll never forget."

Epilogue. It was only years later that I, like Jung, could finally
embrace this experience and write the above poem. It was, for
me, a form of grace.

Embracing Job

...truth comes into this world with two faces.
One is sad with suffering, and the other laughs,
but it is the same face...

—J. G. Neihardt (2000, 145)

Once upon a time in a very ancient land
there lived a "blameless and upright man."
His name was Job, a darling son of God
(but Satan challenged this view).
O, you've probably heard this story,
but have you understood it?

We are told that God permits Job to suffer
at Satan's hands to test his true piety.
He loses all his wealth, then his children.
And Job said, "The Lord has given, and
the Lord has taken away,
blessed be the name of the Lord."

But God and Satan were not finished.
Job's body was totally inflamed.
Even his wife urged him to curse God.
And Job said, "Should we accept only good
from God and not accept evil?"
Still Job was pious and without sin.

But he despaired, even of his very existence,
that offered "no repose, no quiet, no rest."
Then Job's friends came to him and said,
"Do not reject the discipline of the Almighty."
"Surely God does not despise the blameless."
"And do not let injustice reside in your tent."

How would you have responded when
Job maintained, "I am blameless—
I am distraught?" Or when he said,
"Yet I will argue my case before Him.
In this too is my salvation: That no
impious man can come into His presence?"

What would you say if it were you?
And Job said to his friends,
"You are all mischievous comforters."
Then he revealed the two truths to them:
"Fear of the Lord is wisdom;
To shun evil is understanding."

Finally, God answered Job
listing His awesome powers
in a tempest of fearsome questions.
"Would you impugn My justice?
Would you condemn Me
that you may be right?"

Well, Job knew you always submit
to a Higher Power, so he did in his reply.
And Job said to the Lord,
"Indeed, I spoke without understanding
but now I see You with my eyes;
therefore, I recant and relent."

God recognized the "truth" Job spoke.
And so He ended Job's suffering.
After Job prayed for his misinformed friends,
God resurrected his life of material wealth.
Then all his relatives and "former friends"
"consoled and comforted him."

"Remember to Fight the Dragon"

—Steve Bond

Two of my most memorable activities during the summer of 2006 were the New York Jung Foundation's program on "Seeking, Losing and Finding Our Way" in early July and learning Transcendental Meditation, or TM, in late August. The last session of the Jung course was a daylong exploration with the author D. Stephenson Bond of his book *The Archetype of Renewal: Psychological Reflections on the Aging, Death and Rebirth of the King.* Bond talked about finding meaning both as individuals and as a society. To do this, he emphasized that we had to be willing to confront and overcome our fears, our inner dragon. He even inscribed my copy of his book with that message. I thought, "How can we recognize the real dragon?"

The answer was soon to be provided by TM. Twice every day I was instructed to meditate for twenty minutes, focusing on my own secret mantra. About a week after I finished the seven-hour course of instruction, I fell into a meditative trance and was immediately conveyed underground as if I were on a subway track. Suddenly, a very bright white light appeared before me. I slowly approached the light and finally entered into it. It was warm and soothing—a union of all colors, emotions, and thoughts. I felt an ecstasy of compassion and overflowing love.

The circle of light encasing me gradually diminished. I looked out and saw a fierce dragon coming toward me. It was attacking me, but I had no fear. The love I felt embraced the dragon, and it became part of me. My father, who'd died fifteen years earlier, replaced it. A flood of questions arose in a semipoetic form.

Questions for My Father

These are the questions
that I carry—
your legacy, my burden.
Can we finally talk?

Did you mean to:
harm me,
the kitchen knife raised,
as you chased me all those time?

Abandon me,
endless hours waiting
alone in the car,
as you illegally opened your store?

Reject me,
grabbing the broom,
while screaming,
"Can't you even sweep properly!"

Deny my manhood,
as I received my PhD,
saying, "Five years and
you're not a real doctor!"

Oh, I wanted answers, but
your doctor left for Passover.
Then you, a firstborn,
were also gone—forever.

My father then answered my questions: "No, I never meant
those things; I love you." And he took the hand of the small
child—me. My mother then joined him. She, too, had passed
away. She gently wiped away the shit from the diaper she had

pushed on my face when I was four. She said, "I'm so sorry. I didn't really mean it. I love you, too." The child I was then walked away hand in hand with his mother and father. They now saw how their wounds had left me with negative father- and mother-complexes. Even though they had divorced after thirty-six years of marriage, my parents now seemed to have found the love and peace that had so eluded them in life. My eyes filled with tears as all this passed before me. I felt healed and renewed from my confrontation with the dragon.

Epilogue. One always has to "remember to fight the dragon." It can appear suddenly in other settings. For example, I brought a poem into our poetry-reading workshop. A woman who always seems to press my buttons made a very hostile, negative remark. "Her poems are all the same!" she exclaimed and went on to further denigrate both the poet and indirectly me for distributing it to the class. "What a putdown! Poor *me*!" I thought. Then another person, a man, piled on by saying that this poem was depressing. Ah, the wounds! I was totally thrown off guard and came home dejected, ready to drop out of the group.

After mulling this over, I suddenly realized that I was giving in to the lingering effects of my negative parental complexes, letting them take control, and not being able to endure the dragons of life's inevitable conflict. The woman and the man were my mother and father dragons, once again trying to rub shit in my face. So every day we may encounter dragons lying in wait for us in the most unsuspecting places—like an innocent poetry class. If we can shine the light of consciousness on them and fully embrace them, we will be free of our complex.

An Encounter with the Mother-Complex

the mother always plays an active part in the origin of the [mother-complex] ...this constellates archetypes which, in their turn, produce fantasies that come between the child and its mother as an alien and often frightening element.

—C, G. Jung, The Mother-Complex (1968, 85)

In August 2006, my wife and I left on a three-week vacation. During that time we had the opportunity to visit with an old friend, Sophia (name changed), who had moved to the area near our destination. She and her husband had new jobs and a new home. They invited us for an overnight visit. Little did I realize that the visit would be an inner encounter and dialogue about dreams and complexes.

Sophia had just finished a book and told us how abandoned she felt by her publisher. Many promises had been made and then not kept. It had thrown her into a major complex as it evoked nearly forgotten memories of how her mother had treated her as a young girl. Tears welled up in Sophia's eyes as she recounted the details of disappointment and the despair it had plunged her into. I immediately felt very connected to her as it reminded me of my own experiences with my father.

We talked about complexes and Sophia revealed how, as a child, she had the image of a monster pursuing her. She hid in the bathroom, holding the door to keep the monster from possessing her. As it attempted to push open the door, she heard it say, "Sophia let me in; it's your mother." This original wound was still with her, and she had coped by living a highly successful life as an independent professional woman. Now her publisher had evoked that wound. It had taken her three months to work through the hurt, to reengage her publisher, and to assert her independence by networking with professional acquaintances to promote her book.

She, as Jung would agree, wanted to feel comfortable with, and even embrace, her complex. Later that evening, we drove to a gelato store for dessert. Suddenly, she became obsessed with her husband's choice of gelato. It contained some nuts, and he was severely allergic to some varieties. Sophia, who is usually calm and controlled, was absolutely possessed by the fear that it might be harmful and was nearly hysterical in demanding that he not eat the gelato. My wife tried to resolve the conflict—first, by grabbing his gelato and then persuading him to go back to the store to buy another, non-nutty flavor. He confided, as they went back together, "I've never seen her act like that." He had triggered, either inadvertently or subconsciously, the other side of her mother-complex—the overprotective, almost smothering side.

When we returned home, I told Sophia that she might have an interesting dream given our intense interactions. That night, not only did Sophia have a significant dream, but I did as well.

Sophia's dream involved a visit to her publisher where absolutely nothing was clear. She didn't understand the language they were speaking nor the information they provided. All she learned was that they wanted her to travel to some unspecified destination. She reacted calmly to all of this and graciously accepted the travel request, even though she had told us the previous evening how she'd been declining all such travel invitations to promote her book so that she could focus on her research work.

Sophia's dream was clearly about her mother-complex. It showed that she was actually out of her complex and still on the journey with her book. While she may not fully know what will happen, she was not giving up. I sent her the following e-mail the next day to underscore this and a related issue:

Sophia, I also wanted to share two brief observations—one on your dream, and the other on your earlier vision of your mother as a monster. In your dream it was great that you were not being judgmental (which is one of Jung's personality dimensions). Not being judgmental about how your publisher is treating you accomplishes two important things: it recognizes that your book is still "a work in progress" with respect to how well it will do; and it keeps you from your complex of being abandoned. My second observation concerning your image of your mother indicates the task confronting you. Like my own with my father (complex) where I needed to recapture some of the "inner masculine" energy that he kept from me, you may also need to take back the "inner feminine" denied you by your frightening mother. I think this process may already be occurring in the e-mails you've been receiving from those benefiting from your book. They are saying you're the good mother, as my own dream clued me in that I was a good father. Hope this is helpful.

Love, Paul

To which she responded:

Paul, thank you for all your insights, which have buoyed me in my journey. I also want to thank you for the warm and caring way you looked at me as I was telling my "tale of woe"—it made me feel so understood and supported.

Love, Sophia

My dream was a bit more complicated than Sophia's, but it also dealt with a complex.

Steam/Scream Dream

I noticed some columns of steam coming up through an oriental carpet in the hallway of our home. I pointed this out to Camille, who said, "Oh, don't worry about it." I was taken aback, especially given her house complex. I said I'd go to the basement to investigate it. I was astonished to find that it was the formerly dank and dingy space from my childhood and had been totally transformed. It was suffused with the most soothing white light that illuminated a totally modern laundry room enclosed in Plexiglas and filled with modern, stainless steel machinery. I thought the owner had rehabilitated the space since my last visit. Nevertheless, the machines were laboring quite hard and giving off the steam.

I returned upstairs where I heard a voice calling down. I asked Camille, "Who's that? And what's she saying?" Camille informed me that we had a guest, Maria Calderone, but that she also couldn't make out Maria's words. I went closer and heard Maria calling down, "I need more hot water!" I told Camille I couldn't handle all this— steam, strangers in the house. I was going to scream. "No, you can't do that," she said. I started to scream anyway. Camille began to hum to drown out my scream, and then put her hand over my mouth.

At that point the scene suddenly shifted. I found myself alone outside in the night where I decided now I can scream. As I was about to do that, I became aware that I was sitting in a wheelchair with my arms and legs twitching. I then had the thought, if you really do start screaming, it will make you crazy.

I then woke up.

My dream indicated the destructive power of the complex. I had just finished reading the section in Maria Tonkiss's (2006) book ¡Adelante! about her horrific father. Even a refurbished unconscious—my new basement—could be overwhelmed by such a complex which I also had and require active intervention as my wife did with the gelato and then in my dream. The consequences of falling into a complex were provided in the final scene of my dream where I'm incapacitated in a wheelchair and being irrational.

I clearly was feeling a great amount of discomfort during my visit with Sophia and her husband. My dream was telling me that I literally needed to ventilate—both with the steam and the scream. In dealing with such complexed behavior, it is always useful to ask, *Why was this?* In retrospect, it was clear both to me and to Camille that Sophia's husband seemed very uncomfortable and distracted. He was late picking us up at the train station, made wrong turns every time he drove us anywhere, wanted us to watch TV after dinner, and left us for over an hour when Sophia said she just wanted to talk. When we went on a morning walk, he again left us to run an errand to his nearby office, and then acted very impatient when he returned. In short, he was the rejecting father arousing my complex.

Epilogue. Sophia and her husband invited us to meet them for dinner in New York City a few months later. Camille tactfully asked him, "You seemed stressed last time we were together. Were you?" He said he was under immense pressure due to two consecutive events he was in charge of at the university where he'd recently taken a new position.

6 Family

Andrew's Secrets

[During] the period of youth [which] extends roughly from the years just after puberty to middle life...we are forced to limit ourselves to the attainable, and to differentiate particular aptitudes in which the socially effective individual discovers his true self.

—C.G. Jung (1969c, 391, 394)

My son, Jeremy, celebrated his twenty-third birthday, on August 2, 2006. He and his wife, Katie, came up from Philadelphia for the weekend to hang out with his brother, Andrew, who joined us for dinner at Le Soir on Saturday. During the meal, Andrew mentioned he'd kept many secrets from us. While Camille seemed annoyed, my mind flashed back.

Could he be referring to the Brownie baking incident? We'd caught him making them downstairs in our basement apartment where he'd absent-mindedly locked himself out and almost burned down the house. Was there more to it than that? Or was he referring to the mushroom machine he agreed to keep for his high school friends? They were going to sell them extolling their supposedly psychedelic properties. I remember hearing the low, strange hum that nobody else seemed to notice. Finally, I traced it to Andrew's bedroom closet. There, buried under layers of blankets just about to overheat and explode, was a machine containing a garden of mushrooms. I quickly removed and disposed of it despite my son's protestations that it had cost his friends about $200. Camille also was mad at me for destroying it because she's a mushroom fancier.

Then I recalled a more positive experience. Could Andrew be referring to the time he hid Alba Garcia in the basement apartment for over a week? Did something else happen then? Alba was a foster child who'd come here from El Salvador with her mother. But her mother died suddenly, and her aunt could not take care of her so she was temporarily at a nearby foster home and attending Ward Melville High School with Andrew. When Alba told Andrew that they were going to send her away to a home in eastern Pennsylvania, he—always the rescuer with a good heart—decided to hide her in our basement. Thank God his confidante and guidance counselor, Barbara O'Leary, persuaded him that this was not only unfeasible but also illegal. Well, I was so moved by Andrew's actions that I wrote the following poem about it.

Security

My computer says
I'm insecure
(and it never even asked).
All that's required
is $29.95 and a download.
No viruses will
get me and
security is mine

Error 1045, 1046,
Error, ERROR!
Security is so
elusive.

My son's friend
is very insecure—
no parents, no relatives.
She's escaped from
her group home;
she's hiding in my basement.

We're wallowing in
insecurity.
The viruses of
the human condition
leave us all
unprotected.

We offer our heart, our hand
amid tears, hugs of farewell.
The social worker says,
"No more letters from your son."
They may, after all,
contain a virus.

Security is so
confining,
and I can only think
ERROR!

Epilogue. Andrew maintained contact with Alba, visiting her twice in Pennsylvania where she finished high school and, for a few years thereafter, here on Long Island where she now lives with her boyfriend and child. But perhaps the greatest secret of, and for, all was that this experience would lead Andrew to pursue a career in social work eight years later.

Quaternity

Remarkably enough, the psychic images of wholeness which are spontaneously produced by the unconscious, the symbols of the self in mandala form, also have a mathematical structure. They are as a rule quaternities (or their multiples).

—C. G. Jung (1969d, 456-457)

The Jungian quarternity, or fourfoldness, occurred on my birthday—66 in 6-06. More precisely, I turned sixty-six years old in June 2006. I was immediately struck by the four sixes, but that was followed by the four amazing gifts I received over the four days between my birthday on June 14 and Father's Day on June 18. The four gifts came from my family—my wife and my two sons.

The first gift, from Camille, was appropriately Jungian in nature. It was a week at the Jung Foundation's Intensive Program on "Seeking, Losing, and Finding Our Way" in New York City, from July 9 through July 14. (Hmm, was there a hidden message here?) The second gift from my older son Jer was a new family member—our soon to be daughter-in-law, Katie. (The wedding occurred July 1 and is described next.) The third gift from Andrew, who had transferred to Stony Brook University that year, was a set of cards—one containing a birthday message; the other, a Father's Day drawing of stained-glass-like artistry. The message said,

Dad,

I cannot express in words my overall admiration, respect, and gratitude for how helpful and supportive you've been to me since I've been home. Being here, while not always perfect, has given me the opportunity to spend time with you; to witness first-hand what a compassionate and dedicated husband and father you are. I couldn't hope to be anything more, and I wouldn't trade this past year for any-thing.

Love,
Andrew

The fourth and final gift of the quaternity came on the Sunday morning of Father's Day. I awoke to find the first stirrings of a poem in my head as Camille slept next to me. I was tempted to arise quickly and start writing, but something in the poem kept me lingering in the bed nestled with my wife. As we cuddled, the stanzas revealed themselves. I felt as if Robert Browning himself was channeling a poem directly to me—a present from the muse who had been absent too long. Here is the lyric poem as it fully emerged.

Linger

Linger in the bed with me
as the hours are twinkling by.
Kiss me, kiss me, kiss me
for tomorrow we can cry.

Linger in the bed with me
as the seasons caress the sky.
Hold me, hold me, hold me
now's not the time for "why."

Linger in the bed with me
as the years are piled high.
Love me, love me, love me
there's eternity to say good-bye.

And so, my family of four (including myself) presented me with four memorable gifts. Camille always says it's psychologically healthy to write down every day those few things you are grateful for. Gratitude is a great gift we too often neglect. And when it comes as a quaternity of four gifts, it is to be savored for a lifetime.

Epilogue. Less than a year later, on Wednesday, April 25, 2007 Andrew presented his Senior Honors Thesis at a poster session celebrating undergraduate research at Stony Brook University. It was a fifth gift—the perfection of the Jungian quintessence!

Andrew Wortman with his research poster

My Son's Big, Fun Wedding

This last part of my life is the best, in excess of anything I could have deserved.

—T. S. Eliot

On July 1, 2006, my oldest son, Jer, married Katherine Waite in Cincinnati, almost exactly four years since I first heard about Katie. Jer had finished his freshman year at my second alma mater Carnegie Mellon University (CMU) where I had met Camille. His record was spectacular—a perfect 4.0. So Camille and I didn't begrudge spending $4,500 to send him back to Spain, where he'd studied the previous summer, to become completely fluent in Spanish. As soon as he arrived, we knew something was afoot. He kept calling to tell us how unhappy he was and that he wasn't sure he'd complete the four-week program. Finally, he called us and said he'd be coming home. "Why?" we asked. It was then that he informed us about Katie.

Jer had spotted her his first day at CMU on the riverboat cruise, but Katie was not interested. She had a boyfriend back home. So, Jer pined and then pursued and his persistence was rewarded just as it had been with his course work. A friendship developed and finally Katie relented to a closer relationship, but only on the condition that Jer leave Spain and join her immediately in Cincinnati.

Needless to say, I was not happy to lose all that money to what I assumed would be a passing romance. After all, Jer had never even dated seriously in high school. But I kept my skepticism to myself, even when I met Katie and learned that she was on a first-name basis with the Tiffany's sales staff and that her current ambition was to be president of her sorority, Delta Gamma. It didn't help that her parents were divorced and that she had a severely autistic younger brother whom she would eventually have to care for. I knew firsthand, however, that interference is not only unappreciated but can also sour relationships. You see, after I'd introduced Camille to my family, my mother had called to tell me not to marry her, unaware that Camille was also on the line! But twenty years later, my mother apologized to Camille and finally acknowledged that she made me happy.

As their college years went by, that Jer was as serious about Katie as she was about him became clear. I was pleased to see how happy she made him, and was amazed at how his brilliance affected her. Her grades went from a B average to an A; she even stepped down from all her major sorority commitments. As for Tiffany's, we all took the mandatory tour of the New York City store with her, but by then I realized that jewelry was part of Katie's artistic side. She made jewelry and even gave Camille a gift of earrings. Both of the engagement and wedding rings were finally purchased by Jer locally. We visited many area jewelry stores as Jer demonstrated his intellect by becoming an instant gem expert, even being able to spot flaws looking through a microscope. Katie and her dad visited us over Christmas 2004, and it was then that Jer proposed.

Now, a year after their graduation, during which Jer completed his premed courses at Bryn Mawr, we were off to the wedding in Cincinnati. The limo arrived on Thursday afternoon, June 29, to whisk us to LaGuardia. Well, plane trips, like life as T. S. Eliot noted, often have a bumpy beginning but hopefully a happy landing. As usual, I had entrusted all the travel arrangements to Camille, who's a veteran and frequent traveler. The first inkling that something was amiss with our tickets came when the curbside attendant said there was a problem and that we'd have to speak to a supervisor. So, we took all our bags inside and waited in line. Finally, Angela Gibson, the Delta supervisor, explained that our tickets weren't valid. It seems that Camille had entered the credit card information incorrectly and had not noticed the request for a correction before the sale was complete.

We all had a collective feeling of temporary helplessness when Ms. Gibson said the flight to Cincinnati was completely sold out. I immediately inquired about flying to nearby Columbus and was told that we could book a round-trip for $1,500 per person. We explained that we would miss our son's wedding if we couldn't get to Cincinnati. When she heard that, Ms. Gibson lived up to her first name (Angela). She immediately found room for us on the Delta flight to Cincinnati and honored the original booking price, $334 per person, round-trip.

We arrived at the Cincinnati airport that is actually in Covington, Kentucky and then headed to the northern suburbs an hour away. Camille had decided we should have a late meal at a local Cincinnati landmark called Skyline Chili. They had a branch a few blocks from our hotel and Camille, whose birthday is July 2, had planned to take all her Pittsburgh relatives there for a birthday lunch on Sunday, the day after the wedding. Well, both Mapquest and the rental car's navigation system could not locate the chili parlor. We did, however, notice our hotel as we futilely followed the Mapquest printout. I decided to go in and get directions. That worked and we were soon having a midnight meal of Cincinnati-style chili that basically consists of chili dished over spaghetti and topped with cheddar cheese. Sounds awful, but Camille found out that they use a secret ingredient—chocolate, and it tasted great!

With dinner out of the way, we checked in and prepared for Friday's events—a trip to the nearby beauty parlor for Camille and the bridal party, the afternoon wedding rehearsal, and then the rehearsal dinner—the one major obligation of the groom's parents. The rehearsal dinner was the highlight of the three-day event for me. It would be small and intimate, especially compared to the nearly two-hundred-person wedding, and was held at local Italian restaurant famous for their pizzas. (Ah, the apple dessert pizza is to die for!) My big challenge was to write a toast to the bride and groom. I agonized over this, but one morning, I had an inspirational image that resulted in the following toast.

The Redwood and the Reed

I want to start with a short story. It is a brief, allegory of the redwood and the reed. Even though I just wrote it, you may still recognize its symbolic meaning. This particular redwood was young, but already quite tall; and the reed was equally young, but delicate, even slender, and quite charming. The reed liked the strong shelter provided by the redwood. And the redwood liked the way the reed nestled next to him.

But, he boasted, "You sweet, small reed cannot see out across the world like I can. My head can peer over mountains, and it nearly brushes the clouds. I can even talk to eagles if I wish."

The reed found all this very interesting. She replied, "Dear redwood, you may see only the sky, but I embrace the earth which holds you tight in its grip as well. I can talk to the flowers, the deer, the rabbits, and the butterflies. You may see far, but I can see what is happening now."

And so they formed a bond, each supporting the other with their vision of the world. And the redwood grew even taller and stronger. And the reed, too, flourished in his protective shade. Soon she blossomed and became a magnificent orchid. People came from all over to see the mighty redwood and the beautiful orchid. They were overcome with his quiet strength and her sweet fragility. They offered them their lasting admiration and affection.

And so I, too, come in admiration and affection to offer a toast to the wonderful redwood—my son, Jer, and to the stunning orchid—his steadfast companion, and my soon-to-be daughter-in-law, Katie, "May the soil of life enrich you both with enduring love."

Camille told me that my delivery was fantastic, and both Jer and Katie loved it. I was glad because I wanted, in Jungian fashion, to capture the archetypal aspects of their union or *hieros-gamos,* as Jung would call it. Moreover, Camille had prepared a special scrapbook with photos of both Jer and Katie at various ages that concluded with my toast. Copies were presented to them and their parents at the rehearsal dinner.

The next day, Saturday, was the big event. It was a very hot (about 97 degrees), sun-soaked day, and I had to wear a black tux. We were instructed to arrive over two hours before the wedding for pictures and an interview with the crew video-taping the events. Everything was perfect—no faulty tickets, or improper directions. The wedding planner and my soon-to-be daughter-in-law had it all under control. I wandered about for two hours, waiting for the ceremony to begin. Shortly after 6 p.m., my wife and I were the first of the wedding party to walk down the aisle to our seats in the front row.

The ceremony was held outdoors and went by in a perfect flash of joy and pride. My son, Jer, stood tall and straight under the cupola, sneaking boyish smiles to his bride as the "celebrant," who conducted the service they had selected led them through the ritual. Finally, they each said their vows, my younger son, Andrew, produced the wedding band for Katie, and they were officially married.

Katherine Waite and Jeremy Wortman

Then it was indoors—to air-conditioning! Of course, before the good food, there were the obligatory toasts including the following poem by me.

Quintet

We could only wonder
  at the joy
for all we heard was
  "It's a boy!"

Life moved on
  in a swirl,
but often we wondered
  about the girl.

Jer and Andrew were
  our sole delights
at least in those moments
  between their fights.

And Jer grew up
  a seeker of knowledge.
In Pittsburgh he found
  just the right college.

Then suddenly came word
  he'd found a lady,
and now we embrace
  our daughter, Katie.

And so, I offer this wedding toast to the newest Mr. and Mrs. Wortman: "May your years together be filled with happiness—and maybe, just maybe, will you be blessed even sooner with a daughter of your own."

A sentimental, and yes, perhaps even a cheesy, poem as one friend commented, but it was how I felt. It was also Jungian in its theme of five, the "quintessence" that Jung thought went even beyond the perfection of the "quaternity" of four. Then, of course, there was the usual fatherly projection of needs onto the son.

With the toasts and dinner over, it was time to socialize with relatives, and maybe even dance. Before I could succumb to my inertia and indecision about joining the youthful throng on the dance floor, my good friend, and fellow Jungian, Elaine Aron grabbed my arm and literally dragged me into the vibrating, swaying mass performing God only knows what current dance. Well, I wasn't called "Slats" for nothing in my own rock 'n' roll youth and soon was steppin' out to the instructions of the deejay. With the heavy black tux, it wasn't long before I was reduced to a puddle of sweat and ready to return to my seat in happy exhaustion.

At that moment, Camille joined me for a slow dance that morphed into a contest to find the couple that had been married the longest. As the deejay instructed couples who been married five, ten, fifteen, twenty years to leave the floor, I thought, with our fortieth anniversary looming, we're going to win this. As the floor emptied, it revealed one other couple, Katie's grandfather and grandmother, who'd been married for sixty-one years! The old surgeon had managed to limp out onto the dance floor, to swing and sway (like Sammy Kaye) with, as he said, "the still one love of his life," and claim his prize.

The night unfolded in socializing with my sons, my younger brother, and my wife's Pittsburgh relatives. Jer chose not to leave early, as is the prerogative of the new bride and groom, but personally to thank all the guests for coming. Toward the end, my sister-in-law's husband approached me with a complaint. He was quite concerned about the sexy, young blonde woman in the provocative red dress. "Who wears a red dress to a wedding?" he asked me, hoping for confirmation of his conservative Christian beliefs. Like a good Jungian, I avoided the obvious Freudian interpretation of his "reaction formation" defense mechanism. Sure she was, as they say, "hot," but she was also Andrew's date who'd driven all the way from Cleveland. I just told him that I found her quite attractive, red, life affirming and that weddings are fun, sexy events. It also turned out that she was as conservative in her religious beliefs, if not dress, as he was.

So, the wedding ended in pleasant, exhilarating relief. Jer and Katie were staying over for Camille's birthday events the next day before leaving for their honeymoon in Varenna, Italy, on Lake Como. It's the most romantic place Camille and I have ever been, and we'd arranged for them to go there.

The Turning Point: Quaternity Redux

[Quaternities] not only express order, they also create it. That is why they generally appear in times of psychic disorientation...

—C. G. Jung (1969d, 457)

As the world wheels through the heavens, events like planets often line up in once-in-a-lifetime conjunctions. December 1, 2008, was just such a day. The big astronomical news was the alignment of the moon with the planets Jupiter and Venus in a gigantic celestial frown. I even ventured out into the chilly night air, but could not spot this unusual trinity. Instead, I was basking in the inner convergence of major events representing a truly unique conjunction of turning points in four recent stressful, but distinct ongoing problems. For Jung, three is merely the precursor of the perfection of four, which he called "the quaternity" (see previous section on that topic).

The events unfolded as follows during the day:

7:45 a.m. Camille and I are up and ready to have breakfast with Andrew, who has to be in district court in Central Islip by 9:30 a.m. Andrew's friend, who has a history of childhood abuse and violent, destructive behavior, had smashed Andrew's personal property and had damaged our house, and then had tried to evade responsibility and turn the tables on him by having Andrew served with an Order of Protection (OOP). Afterward, his now ex-friend had used the OOP to continue to intimidate, threaten, and coerce Andrew.

The breakfast is quiet and focused on other topics, but Andrew, true to his attention-deficit disorder, does not leave enough time to get to the courthouse by 9:00 a.m., where he's to meet his lawyer. I also have to leave to teach the final session of the OLLI workshop, History through Literature, which I had agreed to lead when the previous instructor was injured.

11:45 a.m. I'm done with the workshop. What a relief! It has been so much more work than I ever anticipated—not only the huge amount of reading, but selecting books and preparing discussion materials, including research on the historical events covered. Today is the first day in three months when I won't have to read at least thirty pages. The workshop participants, however, are great—committed, passionate, and involved; they give me a round of applause. This makes it worthwhile. And next term, I'll have six discussion coleaders to share the burden with me.

Noon: I find a voicemail from Camille telling me that Andrew got lost and couldn't find the courthouse. He wasn't able to contact me since my phone was off during my class. Camille sounds distressed, but ends her message with "I just want to hear your voice." I can't reach Andrew and can't call Camille since now she's teaching her class. I find myself having thoughts that emerge as lines of a poem. The only part I remember is *There is no pain like the pain of love.*

2:30 p.m. I phone Camille and agree to meet her at the parking garage so we can go home together (I had taken the bus to school). She is still very distraught. She had hoped the court case might be dismissed, but it has been continued until January 21. The lawyer wants an additional $1,250 (beyond the $1,000 we've already paid him).

4:30 p.m. I return from a much-needed walk around Setauket Harbor and Andrew finally joins us. He doesn't seem at all troubled by the delay in his case. The good news is that Andrew's former friend appeared and asked that all the charges be dropped and the OOP lifted. While the judge decided to keep the OOP in place, I'm quietly happy with that since I worry that Andrew, who is always generous, might forgive his friend and start hanging out with him again. I see the OOP as just the restraint he needs to focus on his GREs and graduate school applications and to give him some distance and space. To me, it's a turning point.

5:00 p.m. Camille places her third call of the day to Bob, a contractor to whom she paid $10,600 in late October as a deposit to re-side our house. She had tried to take the burden off me by handling this latest house problem. Unfortunately after signing the contract, she immediately realized that the siding would be unsightly and then cancelled it within the three business days allowed. However, Bob has been unwilling to return the money despite telling us repeatedly that he's reputable and will do so. Now Bob actually answers the phone and says he'll be over later this week with the first part of the repayment. Camille dances a jig around the kitchen, rejoicing at another turning point in our ongoing house trauma.

6:30 p.m. Rhoda Spinner calls. She's been thinking about Andrew (bless her!) and wants to know what happened. I bring her up to date, but really want to know how her Thanksgiving turned out. That was the first time her husband, Joel, has been home since being diagnosed with leukemia just before Labor Day. Camille and I have been part of their support system—providing transportation, emergency meals for Joel, and emotional assistance. For me, this has been especially trying since it evokes the trauma of my older brother's death from pancreatic cancer a decade earlier. I even have a dream revealing this (see the following). But now Joel, after all the ups and downs over the past three months, is in remission and at home. Rhoda sounds absolutely reinvigorated as she recounts how Joel enjoyed Thanksgiving, including the very special bottle of merlot I promised him, and is back to his usual frenetic, high-energy state—fixing the car and reorganizing his clothes closet. He's even cleaning the dinner dishes as we speak! It's a miracle or, as they say in Yiddish, a *mekhaye!* And it's the fourth, and final, turning point of the day when the conjunction of events dispels the dark, gloom of the inner world.

Journey Dream: Friday, November 28

The following is the dream I had just prior to the events described above. It provides a useful exercise in Jungian dream interpretation, which is presented in a Q-and-A format afterward.

I'm headed toward my car having just visited a place I can't recall. The car really isn't mine, but Camille's. It's a light, silver blue color and is clearly old. There has evidently been a problem with local transportation that prevents others from traveling. As I'm about to get in, I notice two men in work clothes with hard hats are in the front seat. I'm surprised and ask what they want. One replies, "I need to see my wife in Hartford Hospital. Can you take me there?"

I say, "I'm sorry, but I'm late getting back to my wife. I can drop you off a mile up the street from the hospital."

The next thing I know the two grimy men have left only to be replaced by five adults with books and pocketbooks who fill the front and backseats. I start to drive and try to think how I'll retrace my steps and get back. We approach a major intersection, which has two cloverlike clusters of three green signs for highways on both the left and on the right. I think I should go left, but, when I ask, a woman in back shouts, "No, you have to take a right."

I can't readjust the car quickly enough and end up going straight ahead through the intersection. There's a red 4×4 truck in front of me. As I follow it, the road seems to narrow, and then I suddenly notice that we seem to be in a lake with only the small rocks marking the shoulders showing above the water. The truck disappears and I see a tiny island ahead where the road bends to the left that seems to be made up of floating logs and worry that we'll soon be in even deeper water. I say, "I think we should stop and back up even though it's quite a long way back."

A man responds, "No, you have to keep going forward."

The next thing I remember is that we seem to have made it to the other side of the lake, but then I wake up.

Dream Interpretation Exercise

What is the first thing you usually encounter in a dream?

According to Jung, upon entering the unconscious you first encounter the shadow, which is generally repressed, mostly negative, persons or material. In this dream, the two men in work clothes with hard hats are, since I do not know them, shadow figures. The fact that there are two of them represents a doubling, which means that they are important.

What shadow material do the two men represent?

Here you need to ask a question of the dreamer: What would you ask? The only information you are provided is the request, by one of the men, to be taken to Hartford Hospital. Therefore, you'd have to ask the dreamer what (s)he associates with this hospital. Unlike Freud, who would encourage free association or any responses that occur, Jung insisted on such directed associations involving personal, specific connections.

Hartford Hospital generates two responses: it is the place where the dreamer was born and it is where his older brother died of pancreatic cancer. So the shadow figure's request triggers the entire arc of life from birth to death, especially the latter, repressed fear of mortality due to cancer. And this is likely a reaction to the dreamer's encounter with a man his brother's age who also has a very serious life-threatening form of leukemia.

What do the five people who replace the two men represent?

The major clues about these shadow figures are that they have books, fill the space, and that the dreamer has to take them to a destination. This seems to fit with the reading class he agreed to lead, but this hypothesis needs support from other parts of the dream. The number five is important as well. Some Jungians consider it to be the next step, or quintessence, beyond the quaternity of four and therefore to represent perfection.

What do the green signs and the discussion of the direction mean?

As with the two men, there is a doubling here, indicating the importance of the signs or directions. They are, in addition, colored green, which is considered positive or life enhancing. There are three signs, which indicate a nearness to four.

The dreamer wants to go in the Jungian appropriate direction which is left—our more intuitive side, but a woman, perhaps an anima figure, says to go "right." Instead, no turn is made which defers the final decision and ultimate direction. Nevertheless, there is a red truck, which indicates some warning as to how the trip will end.

What does the water on the road mean?

Water is often associated with the unconscious. Here, the water is not too deep, and it is therefore safe to follow the submerged road. This is supported by the disappearance of the red truck, the apparent safety of an island, and the road starting to bend to the left.

A man tells the dreamer to "keep going forward." What does this mean?

The dreamer needs guidance—the major purpose of dreams according to Jung. Here, there is an authoritative male voice. Jung would consider this the Self, that inner, unconscious place of totality and spirituality that is superior to the ego. Such encounters are rare, but always important in their guidance.

There is some uncertainty about whether the journey ends safely. How can the dreamer determine if this is the case?

Jung developed another technique for connecting with the unconscious called *active imagination*. This requires the dreamer to consciously ask a question of a dream character. Here, the dreamer determined that the other side of the lake had, in fact, been reached and a woman passenger requested to be let out at a bus stop, indicating that the destination has been safely achieved.

7 Culture and Politics

Southern Hospitality

It is rather for us to be here dedicated to the great task remaining before us.

—Abraham Lincoln, The Gettysburg Address

I had hit the trifecta. On Friday, August 25, 1967, I successfully defended my dissertation and officially became Dr. Wortman. The next day was my wedding (see I Was Married by the ACLU). We had $125 to spend and made do with vegetable plates; the Carnegie Mellon University chapel (free); a harpsichord (loaned by a friend); a harpsichord player—Krishnahadi Pribadi, the Indonesian renaissance student and former suitor of my soon-to-be wife; and no clergy since under Pennsylvania law anyone can use the Quaker form of marriage (so much for separation of church and state). So, we said our vows, which we had carefully scripted, and married ourselves.

On the third day, Sunday, there was no rest as we drove off from Pittsburgh in our gleaming new blue Dodge to my first full-time job as an assistant professor of psychology at Duke University in Durham, North Carolina. I had wrestled between choosing an academic career as a psychologist or using my extensive computer skills (I was fluent in eleven different computer languages) in applied, corporate research. For reasons I now understand (see You're an INFP), I chose the academy.

Camille, however, was not thrilled to be heading south to complete her undergraduate studies at Duke. She had a standing offer from Hanna Holborn Gray, then president of the University of Chicago, for a full-scholarship there. My faculty mentors thought Duke was the best job any one of their students had ever obtained, and thus, they'd only made perfunctory inquiries into Chicago-area schools.

We arrived in Durham that same day. It was the first time I'd seen it in daylight, having been intentionally flown in for my job interview at night. It was small after Pittsburgh—dominated by the massive, redbrick Liggett & Myers Chesterfield cigarette factory and more X-rated movie theaters than I'd seen since visiting Times Square. It was the first inkling of the effects of Bible Belt repression that characterizes the South. That fall, Camille had to take a required two-semester undergraduate course, Jesus, the Man and His Message.

The next day we went to the Duke campus, where I met the head secretary of psychology, Ms. Amby Peach. How perfectly southern she was, not only in name but complete with the honeyed charm covering an iron-fisted, authoritative personality also. Ms. Peach directed us to the Duke Housing Office. There we were given a thick book with handwritten listings. Just about each one had a large red star next to it. Camille asked, "What does the red star mean?" She was told, "Whites only." We stood there in shock.

A century after the Civil War, over a decade after the Supreme Court outlawed segregation, seven years after the sit-ins down Tobacco Road in Greensboro, and just a few years after Lyndon Johnson signed the Voting Rights Act, we were confronted with the ugly remnants of Jim Crow enforced by a major university. Should we defer to such racism? Did we have any choice? Signs displayed in restaurant windows advertised "Help Wanted. Whites Only" and even *The Durham Morning Herald* advertised in its Positions Wanted "Whites Only."

Eventually, we rented a small bungalow in the northern part of Durham. Our landlords, the Wilkins, extended the usual Southern hospitality and invited us over for dinner at their stately home nestled on the outskirts in the Duke forest. During the dinner, Mr. Wilkins asked to be excused for a moment. The next thing we heard was the earsplitting report of what turned out to be a shotgun blast. When Mr. Wilkins returned, we asked what had happened. He said his dog had treed a stray cat in the yard, and he'd shot it!

These were the Wallace years; the next spring Martin Luther King was assassinated just over the state line in Memphis; Jesse Helms, then a commentator on WRAL-TV, opined that Dr. King had got what he deserved; and guns were omnipresent in the racks behind the windows of many 4×4s. We decided to explore the state and headed off to the Coastal Plain and the Outer Banks. Just past Raleigh, we were greeted by a huge red billboard with a picture of a black knight in armor astride a black horse. With his visor down and lance forward, the knight seemed intent on impaling time itself as his message read "Impeach Earl Warren. Stamp out desegregation. United Klans of America." It was just as Thurgood Marshall had teasingly said to the young, black psychologist Kenneth Clark, as they headed south fifteen years earlier to collect the data that would overturn de jure segregation. When Clark, who'd never been in the South, nervously inquired if they'd crossed the Mason–Dixon line, Marshall replied (Simple justice, 1993), "Oh yes. We're in Nuth Car'linah. We've crossed the Smith and Wesson line!"

Epilogue. Some forty years later—after the coming and then passing of that modern-day Senator Bilbo, Jesse Helms—the world changed yet again. On Tuesday, November 4, 2008, a young African-American, in the truest sense of the word, Barack Obama, was elected the forty-fourth president of the United States. The last state he carried was North Carolina.

A few months earlier I had written the following letter to *The New York Times*:

To the Editor:

Re "After Grueling Battle, Obama Claims Nomination" (front page, June 4):

The nomination of Barack Obama by the Democratic Party is truly a historic moment. For those, like me, who can remember the Brown v. Board of Education Supreme Court decision, school integration battles in Little Rock, Ark., the sit-ins in Greensboro, N.C., the Rev. Dr. Martin Luther King's March on Washington and the Voting Rights Act, it is absolutely amazing.

All Americans—black and white, men and women, Northerners and Southerners— should pause along with the candidate to reflect on the significance of this event. It marks yet another major step in the redemption of America's soul from its dark legacy of slavery and Jim Crow bigotry, and its fulfillment of, as Mr. Obama often says, hope for a better life for all.

Published by *The New York Times* on June 5, 2008

Celebrating the Obama victory

Sitting: Ed and Ellen O'Neal, the author and Camille

Willy, Jim and Dave

An aged man is but a paltry thing,
A tattered coat upon a stick, unless
Soul clap its hands and sing, and louder sing
For every tatter in its mortal dress,

—W. B. Yeats (1996), "Sailing to Byzantium"

On June 14, 2009, I turned sixty-nine. It was time to start planning for the Big 7-0! For my sixtieth, everything seemed just to fall into place. I was active in poetry—both reading and writing. And my favorite poet was (and still is) William Butler Yeats, who was born on June 13 in western Ireland. Moreover, thanks to another Irishman, Professor Paul Dolan, I'd just finished reading James Joyce's *Ulysses* (1990). In fact to be honest, I'd persuaded Professor Dolan, whose undergraduate course on Yeats I'd loved, to offer one covering both Homer's *Odyssey* and Joyce's classic revision of it that takes place in Dublin on June 16, the date he met his future wife, Nora Barnacle.

Yeats (1996, 249-250*) had written of the Jungian "tension of opposites" in his poem, "Vacillation:"

> Between the extremities
> Man runs his course;
> A brand, or flaming breath,
> Comes to destroy all those antinomies
> Of day and night;
> The body calls it death,
> The heart remorse.
> But if these be right
> What is joy?

And Joyce (1990, 783) provided an answer by having Molly Bloom conclude her famous stream-of-consciousness soliloquy (which also ends the journey of her husband, Leopold) with

> ....and then I asked him with my eyes to ask again yes and then he asked me would I yes to say yes my mountain flower and first I put my arms around him yes and drew him down to me so he could feel my breasts all perfume yes and his heart was going like mad and yes I said yes I will Yes.

So, I had no choice but to say yes to Ireland and to being embraced by these two literary giants on my sixtieth birthday. It was an odyssey of joy and, although I was not fully aware of it at the time, the true beginning of my Jungian journey of restoration, for if ever there was a Jungian poet, it was his contemporary, Willy Yeats. Like Jung he lived part-time in a tower writing poetically, as only the Irish can, of the tensions between despair and elation—always searching for meaning that would allow him to become a "finished man."

Camille and I flew into Shannon and then took the bus to our first destination, Galway. We'd planned to take buses rather than risk driving on the left-hand side of the narrow Irish roads. At least, that's what I thought, but evidently Camille was not so sure. When we checked in to Jury's Inn, she noticed a small ad for a local, personal tour driver pinned to the bulletin board. The driver's name was David Hogan, and he lived just outside Galway in Kinvara. She, like Molly Bloom, persuaded me to say yes to her calling about his fees to take us to some nearby places. He charged two hundred euros per day, and we needed him for three days. Too much, I thought, but Dave, like Camille, was equally intolerant to no. He offered to take us for a half-day trial at one hundred euros, and we agreed.

The next morning, Dave showed up in his shiny new Toyota Camry and off we went. Our half-day ended eight hours later, after seeing the misty Cliffs of Moher in County Clare; the ancient, prehistoric Celtic burial ground in the nearby moonscape called the Burren; and a medieval cemetery—all accompanied by Dave's irresistible Irish cheer and informative background stories. We hired him for our remaining three days to explore northwestern Ireland.

The following day we visited the ancient Norman tower at Thoor Ballylee near Gort where Yeats lived and wrote both *The Tower* and *The Winding Stair*, his collection of masculine and feminine poems, respectively. On the following day, June 13, Dave drove us to the churchyard cemetery in Drumcliff, County Sligo where Yeats is buried. It was a day just as the poet described in his valedictory poem, "Under Ben Bulben," (Yeats, 1996, 327-328**):

> Flowers and grass and cloudless sky
> Resemble forms that are, or seem
> When sleepers wake and yet still dream,
> And when it's vanished still declare,
> With only bed and bedstead there,
> That Heavens had opened.

The poem concludes with the memorable epitaph chiseled on Yeats's gravestone:

> Cast a cold eye
> On life, on death.
> Horseman, pass by!

Standing like a mourner in that graveyard, I finally realized I had now entered the Jungian second half of life with its admonition so poignantly expressed by Yeats (1996, 250) in the lines from "Vacillation" I'd memorized as an exercise in Professor Dolan's class.

> No longer in Lethean foliage caught
> Begin the preparation for your death

And from the fortieth winter by that thought
Test every work of intellect or faith
And everything that your own hands have wrought,
And call those works extravagance of breath
That are not suited for such men as come
Proud open-eyed and laughing to the tomb.

The next day it was on to Ireland's Wild West, County Donegal, where I had persisted in persuading Dave to drive us to the Slieve League, the highest sea cliff on the Irish mainland and, at almost two thousand feet tall, three times the height of the more famous Cliffs of Moher and that much more spectacular. Finally, after a night celebrating my birthday at Harvey's Point Country Hotel resort, our travels with Dave ended as he dropped us at the bus station in Donegal Town the next morning for our cross country trip to Dublin and the weeklong Bloomsday celebration of Joyce's masterpiece.

Again, it was Yeats (1996, 251)who so beautifully expressed the fleeting nature of these Jungian numinous, truly religious moments where one encounters one's Self.

My fiftieth year had come and gone
I sat, a solitary man,
In a crowded London shop,
An open book and empty cup
On the marble table top.

While on the shop and street I gazed
My body of a sudden blazed;
And twenty minutes more or less
It seemed, so great my happiness,
That I was blessed and could bless.

Upon our return home, I was surprised to find two articles on sightseeing in western Ireland in the Travel section of the Sunday *New York Times*. They claimed that the only way to get around was to rent a car, which is quite difficult since the back roads are often unmarked and filled with monstrous tour buses. It prompted me to write a letter about my trip and how Dave Hogan made it truly memorable. And, with the luck of the Irish, *The New York Times* published it on August 27, 2000.

Needless to say, this letter generated considerable interest in Dave's services, and he escorted quite a lot of happy travelers through the area as a result. Although I have not made it back to Ireland, Dave and I have been in regular contact through both snail mail and e-mail ever since that remarkable odyssey.

September 11, 2006

"The horror! The horror!"

—Joseph Conrad, Heart of Darkness

It's the anniversary of 9/11. I remember that bright, blue morning of promise. It was my first day in The Round Table (now OLLI), the Stony Brook University retirement learning community, and I was excited to be officially retired. At the time the first tower of the World Trade Center (WTC) was struck, I was making my way through the labyrinth of the Main Library to Carl Siegel's course, ironically on Tolstoy's *War and Peace*. As I entered the classroom, I was told the news that a plane had hit the WTC. No one gave it that much thought since it was presumed to be some weird accident. Not until the class ended and I went to the computer shop in the Psychology A Building did I learn the shocking news.

Glenn Hudson, the technician in charge of helping faculty with their computers, informed me that both towers had been attacked and, to my complete astonishment, had collapsed. "They don't exist," he said. I was stunned. I then went to the university computer store where a television was replaying those horrific scenes that are now forever seared in our memory. I stood transfixed, overwhelmed with shock and grief. I had that feeling everyone seemed to have. All our defenses of denial and distraction had been violently ripped away and we were all left confronting our mutual fragility, our vulnerability, and our mortality. In the immense shock and sadness, there also emerged a supportive compassion that everyone shared—even total strangers I encountered.

The scenes—of the plane flying into the second tower, of the tower imploding, and of people fleeing the monstrous white dust cloud as it raced around the corner and down the street after them—were all replayed over and over until we, too, were traumatized with the horror of those moments. The raw feelings of helplessness, anger, and compassion washed over me repeatedly. I tried to come to grips with all of this and let it settle over me just like the dust that caked so many of the victims and survivors. I found, as I often have in the past, that poetry was the best outlet for my feelings. This is what I wrote.

September 11, 2001

In the unconscionable, in the unspeakable, in the
unbearable
please embrace these dust-coated, red remains.
Let us lift them high as prayer into our heavens.
Let us cleanse them free as spirits with our hearts.

In the smoke, in the sorrow, in the shock
please accept these sterile, white scraps.
Let me wrap them tight as love around your wounds.
Let me wipe them quiet as compassion on your tears.

In the aftermath, in the anger, in the adversity
please contemplate these endless blue banners
Let them surround us pure as sky throughout our world.
Let them cool us calm as conscience to true peace.

Here in the red fire of renewal,
here in the white clouds of hope,
here in the blue harbor of liberty,
we join our forefathers in unity, solemnity, and action.

The effects of 9/11 reverberated in me throughout the
following year. I had visited the WTC site with Camille and
a friend in late October, 2001. The blackened, shrouded hulk
of the Deutsche Bank building looming over the rubble was
reminiscent of the destruction from World War II with the
added component of the acrid, nauseating smell of death. The
surrounding fences and barricades were decorated with con-
dolence messages, photos of loved ones, and flowers. Other
poems emerged. I, like so many, was still struggling for closure.

The following summer Camille and I took a short vacation
in Vermont. As it turned out, a quilting convention was being
held nearby, and one of the quilters was staying at the same

resort and had her work on display there. She had an American flag design that immediately struck me as being compatible with my poem. We started talking and soon reached an agreement where she would design a quilt that featured my poem. By the end of the summer, it was complete. I found emotional closure but still would like to donate it to the 9/11 memorial museum when it finally opens.

How else did I spend that day? I could not bear to watch TV. My son warned me that they were replaying all those indelible shocking moments. I had also been forewarned about ABC's attempt to turn fact into fiction with a televised program, and I suspected that President Bush would continue to politicize the day with his own attempt to turn fiction into fact by hyping the connection to Iraq. Instead, I chose to focus on the true compassion of the day as presented in *The New York Times*'s "Portraits of Grief" and the following poem I composed to the victims on the first Memorial Day after 9/11.

In Memoriam Day

Oh my God! Have we
like Icarus climbed too high
that the fireball of the morning sun
rammed our mighty towers?

The heat and smoke
of my charred aspirations
have forced me from
my perch on this blackened wick.

All reason's overwhelmed;
my compass blurred;
the frame of my space unhinged.
Ashen faced, wingless
I tumble through the
gaping wound of this world.

I land—now—forever—
in you. Hold my
memory tight in the
tear-streaked pew
of grief, and
let me rest eternally
in the soft hours we shared
together.

The author with his flag quilt and 9/11 poem

Another Letter for The *Times*

After every war
someone has to tidy up.
...
Someone has to shove
the rubble to the roadsides
so the carts loaded with corpses
can get by.

—Wislawa Szymborska, The End and the Beginning

I'm a compulsive writer of letters to *The New York Times*. On Thursday, May 3, 2007, they published a letter I wrote about President Bush's veto of the Iraq spending bill he'd requested to fund a so-called surge of military forces in Baghdad. I must have written about ten letters that have appeared in The Times by then, but there's a Jungian story behind this particular letter.

I was reading David Lindorff's book *Pauli and Jung: The Meeting of Two Great Minds* (2004) dealing with Jung's analysis of Wolfgang Pauli's many dreams. Pauli, a world-famous theoretical physicist and Nobel laureate, lived in Zurich at the same time as Jung. I had just read about the dream where Pauli had an encounter with the Jungian Self or soul, which admonished him to participate in the world. A voice said, "Woe unto them who use religion as a substitute for the other side of the soul's life; they are in error and will be accursed…Out of the fullness of life shall you bring forth your religion; only then shall you be blessed." The dream concluded by noting that Pauli must "feel" this religious experience rather than rely solely on his strong intellect (Lindorff, 2004, 42-43).

So, when I read *the Times*'s front-page story about the Bush veto of the Democrat-sponsored Iraq war–funding bill that contained withdrawal dates and benchmarks, it must have unconsciously clicked with me. The story continued on the page containing the names of the soldiers killed that day. This led to a focus (totally unconscious) on a feeling rather than an intellectual reaction. My initial thought on writing a letter was, "Why bother? Everyone is going to be sending in letters to *The Times* about this." But the admonition in Pauli's dream carried me past that. *Et voila!*

In this letter, I was also consciously trying to take Bush's projections or blaming of others and turn them back upon him. All his projective statements are incredibly self-revelatory. It seems as if the president has to constantly purge (or evacuate) himself of all his terrible impulses by projecting them onto others. We all do that, of course, but Bush's statements are literally self-descriptive gems revealing a very dark shadow-side of his personality.

The other thing I noticed, after the fact (that is, I was unconscious of it), is that the number of military deaths—3344—has immense Jungian significance. First, the number 4 or the Jungian quaternity is a sign of completion--the squaring of the circle or mandala. Second, the doubling of the numbers also signifies that they are important symbols. Third, this may foretell the end of conflict—moving from "3" to the finality of "4." And it did. In July 2010, President Obama ended combat operations in Iraq.

Here's what I wrote.

To the Editor:

As President Bush signed his second veto, you note another seven "Names of the Dead" for a total of

3,344. How many more brave men and women must die before the president and his Congressional allies finally realize that having no exit strategy and no firm benchmarks is the real "prescription for chaos and confusion" in Iraq that mark the ultimate failure of the administration?

The president's continued insistence on a blank check for financing the war after four years is itself completely "irresponsible" and totally unacceptable.

Published by *The New York Times* on May 3, 2007

I shared this with my friend, Elaine Aron, who is an analyst. She validated my approach by saying, "What I notice most is the strong feeling you expressed--the strong emotional words, the clear judgment. I am sure that is what they liked. Forget the long-winded arguments. You cut to the chase: the complete waste of lives. The horror of it comes through."

The Parthenon Marbles

The Parthenon without the marbles is like a smile with a tooth missing.

—Neil Kinnock

On June 20, 2009, the New Acropolis Museum opened in Athens. The museum may soon be famous for what is missing from its collection—the Parthenon, also known as the Elgin, marbles. They are the figures from the frieze of the Parthenon that were removed by the British ambassador, Lord Elgin, in the early nineteenth century when Greece was still part of the Ottoman Empire and the Parthenon was used by the Turks as a munitions depot. Elgin shipped the marbles to England for safekeeping and then sold them to the British Museum in 1816. The Greeks have been trying to get the marbles back. The British Museum had recently offered a three-month loan of the marbles on the condition that Greece acknowledges British ownership. The Greek government declined the offer.

All of this brought back a journey I made to England in early spring 2002. I was on my way to France to hike with some friends. The trip provided a two-day layover in London where I planned to stage a one-man protest at the British Museum in support of the return of the Parthenon marbles. I took the tube to the museum and first visited the new wing housing the marbles. It is a sterile, almost sullen, place with the marbles scattered like forlorn orphans. I then ventured out into the pleasant spring day and joined the few food vendors outside the metal fence near the entrance. There I greeted passersby with, "Would you like a poem?" Most took me up on my offer. I stayed at my post for two hours and only one person (perhaps a descendant of Lord Elgin or a museum employee) politely returned the poem.

The author at the Parthenon

I had written the poem (below) five years earlier during my first trip to Greece and visit to the acropolis. I added my protest message in the left-hand margin as follows.

Healing Athena

Old Zeus is dead;
the Acropolis is finally free of his grasp.
But has mighty Athena fled
leaving only an empty crown?

Help

A wounded monument can still heal
if you ask it.

Athena Heal

I sought elusive Demeter,
but her temple is barren
swallowed in Hades' open jaws—
a dark contemplation of
thoughts lost on an opaque wall.
All words have been ground to silence
leaving worn teeth in rotted gums
choked in the rubble of time.

Support

A wounded monument can still heal
if you hear it.

the Return

I made the long pilgrimage to Delphi.
Its ancient wind still whispers
mysterious, pithy prophecies
sealing the fate of empires.
Gods and men alike sought to possess
the oracle of destiny
only to become destiny's prisoner.
There my ears were confined to solitude.

A wounded monument can still heal
if you cleanse it.

of the

I scoured the dark serpentine alleys.
At Dionysus' boisterous table I sipped
from the cup of joyful nectar;
my soul danced to a bouzouki ballad
with only my tears to embrace.
I floated away on the cool tide of night
a dream for a blanket,
a hope for a pillow.

Parthenon

A wounded monument can still heal
if you let it.

Marbles

The bells of empty churches chattered
as I made the ascent to Athena's temple.
In the warm equal light
of a new sun and full moon
I heard her voice swaddled
in the darkness that has covered all women:
"There is no ideal life,
but there is life of the ideal."

to Greece

Later that same day I penned the following poem about my experiences at the British Museum, sprinkling it with phrases from some famous British poems and dedicated to the Greek women I have met.

At the British Museum

*For Cynthia, Lila, Marina, Vasiliky and all the women of
Greece*

Is this all that's left of their glory—
the broken remnants of empires?
A jigsaw puzzle of heroic plunder
rests here–last testament of their will.
Captives of the past, they lie
immobilized like Hector,
a pirated corpse displayed
as a bitter triumph of dead civilizations.

In this graveyard the soul of Greece wails
while Nelson struts atop his dagger
impaled in the heart of the colossal wreck.
Hear, O royal subjects Athena's cries
for her marvelous garments—
those beauteous forms ripped from her bosom
commemorating democracy's birth.
Here they are found and it's her will
not to yield.

Outside that marble vault,
one hears a stilled heart whisper,
"When will it ever end?"
Then another replies,
"Hurry up please it's time.
We've drunk our draught
and had them long enough."

Jung honored the mythological figures, which he called
"archetypes" that he claimed inhabited the "collective unconscious" of all human beings throughout time. Many of those

archetypes, especially for those of us in the West, originated in ancient Greece. They teach us important lessons that we ignore at our peril. So my brief pilgrimage, protest, and poems also honor that heritage and the healing it can bring us.

8 Anima Issues

Karin

A man who has not passed through the inferno of his passions has never overcome them.

—**C. G. Jung (1989, 277)**

In the fall of 2000, Camille invited a visiting postgraduate student, Karin, from Germany to work with her on a research project. Karin and I met only about a half dozen times—two fall holiday dinners at our home, a farewell trip into Manhattan for dinner and a play that was a gift from Camille, and two or three times when I was in my university office located a few doors away from Karin's and she was passing by. She had a shy, sensitive, wounded gaze with a personality that shaded into self-absorption bordering on vanity. Nevertheless, there was a certain seductive aspect in her demeanor and in her large hazel eyes framed by alabaster skin, lustrous black hair, and an inviting, toothy smile that flashed intermittently like a beckoning buoy on a dark night.

She was the only woman besides Camille who ever penetrated my personal space. To my surprise, she nestled close to me when I showed her around my office, and I was flattered by her interest in both my poetry and research involving new methods for data analysis. This contact seemed to exert an emotional pull that I found both enjoyable and disturbing. She was here for only three months and returned to Germany. I have not seen her since then.

Karin would have been just a pleasant, but passing, memory if she had not stayed in contact with Camille as they worked on a book chapter together. A couple of times I answered the phone and chatted with her until Camille was available. A few months later, I sent Karin an e-mail to see how she was doing with her work that we'd discussed. She was depressed and sought my technical advice on her master's thesis that she was struggling to complete in English. She asked me to read her thesis, to correct the English, and to review her statistical methods. It seemed an innocent enough request, but that initial step toward intimacy almost overwhelmed me.

I soon learned Karin's story of how her first teenage romantic sexual experience had ended in the trauma of betrayal as her best girlfriend had seduced her paramour, and had left her emotionally victimized and unable to form any relationship for the next ten years. It immediately tapped into my still unconscious rescuer-martyr archetype and my own sense of wounded betrayal (see Prologue; Why I Retired). I was being invited into her life and this spark ignited the tinder of my anima, that "inner feminine figure [that] plays a typical, or archetypal role in the unconscious of man" according to Jung. It didn't matter that I was sixty-two and she was twenty-six at the time. It was the beginning of a long exchange over the next years of what Camille called my "e-mail affair."

I felt a sense of alternating fear, fascination, and exhilaration as I, like that modern-day Ulysses, Leopold Bloom, was enthralled with the charms of young Gerty MacDowell (a.k.a. Princess Nausicaa). I was impelled forward in the possession of this energizing anima projection that was so powerful that I could only marvel and then succumb to it. I wrote sweet notes, sent Christmas and birthday cards, and even gifts. I wrote the following poem in an attempt to capture all of this and more.

Our Odyssey

Odysseus, old campaigner, stay no more in my house against your will. But first another journey calls. You must travel down to the House of Death and the awesome one, Persephone...

We came from different times:
She in my future: I before her past.
We came from different places:
she from an ancient land; I from one new.
We came from different cultures:
she from one accomplished,
but weary with history's blood-stained guilt;
I from one struggling for identity
under hubris' brash innocence.

She carried the seeds
of spring's hope.
You can call her Persephone.
I wore the frost
of autumn's wisdom.
You can call me Bloom.

It was in Hades that we met:
our naked souls wallowing
in a clotted sea of suffering;
our mortal remains coated
with the bitterness of betrayal;
our hearts torrid infernos
pulsing in passion's agony.

I reached out a healing hand,
but she held fast for fear
of an ever-changing inner world.
At last she accepted
my amulet of unconditional trust

for the inevitable journey
of return yet to come.

And so we sat in idle communion
while Demeter's crystalline tears
cleansed the wounds of loss
and decorated the earth's surface
with flowering banners of renewal.
We read only simple words
through each other's eyes—
each one a balm of insight.

The "simple words" we decided to share were books. Karin was an avid reader and suggested reading and discussing some novels together. I was stunned by Karin's first choice, *Lolita*. This was clearly way over the top for me in its overt seductiveness. I was not going to let even my now overactive anima drag me there.

Her next choice was nearly as bad—Philip Roth's *The Dying Animal*, about a lecherous, old Jewish professor about my age and his affair with a young, voluptuous female student about Karin's age! Beyond the graphic, often desperate and demeaning sex, a moment of epiphany, hope, and even love, seemed finally to arrive. At the conclusion, the professor compassionately embraces the woman who has lost the breasts he so lusted after to cancer. Could it be that self-acceptance and self-love can or must occur with age and that healing leads to a true love of others? Roth seemed to be saying the instinctual animal must die first for that to happen.

After this, I recommended Gunter Grass's *Crabwalk*, which focused on the sinking of the German ship, Wilhelm Gustloff, near the end of World War II. Over nine thousand civilian refugees perished—the largest maritime disaster in history. Karin read it in German; I in English; and then we compared notes. She even did a small survey and found that, as Grass thought, neither her friends nor her parents had heard of it. I found the novel interesting enough in terms of its narrative style and theme of unexperienced grief and loss to assign it to my History through Literature workshop.

Karin resumed her anima-inflaming choices by then selecting Norman Rush's *Mating*. It turned out to have a similar theme as the Roth book, but in reverse—the young woman pursues and seduces the older man. Ironically, one of Karin's friends upon seeing the cover said I was the one engaged in seduction. I couldn't even finish it as the characters seemed uninteresting and the writing was not engaging, but Karin did. Clearly, two animas (my anima and her animus, our inner or unconscious ideal feminine and masculine figures, respectively) were sending a strong message. But what was it?

I shared all this with Camille, who speculated that perhaps it was some delayed midlife crisis that she called the "poopsie syndrome," where older men need younger women to recapture their youth. I, on the other hand, thought it might be a substitute for teaching and being around young people, which I missed in my retirement. Or, maybe it was a fear of death. But the sheer magnetic, emotional power clearly came from something much deeper. Thinking only led me to dead ends as the power of this feminine force was overwhelming.

I was a psychologist and thus determined to find out the source of this emotional turmoil. I realized, as in the preceding poem, that like Bloom (or Odysseus), I was going to visit the Nighttown (or Hades) of my unconscious and confront the anima figure of Bella Cohen (or Circe). And thus began my inner quest, which evolved slowly into a Jungian journey and my own confrontation with the unconscious.

......

But the anima has a positive aspect as well. It is she who communicates the images of the unconscious to the conscious mind...

—C.G. Jung (1989, 187)

The urgency of understanding and coping with my Karin-inspired anima attack was underscored when I read the following in Frank McLynn's (1996, 304) biography of Jung: "The animus and anima [our ideal feminine and masculine images, respectively] were what Jung called 'archetypes of the soul' and he warned eloquently of the danger that they could irrupt into the conscious, causing schizophrenia or other psychoses." This brought back grim memories of the German movie *The Blue Angel*, where an older professor enamored of a youthful, seductive, cabaret siren, portrayed by Marlene Dietrich, finds that his jealous lust reduces him to a clown and finally to an insane, crowing rooster. So, I took McLynn's admonition seriously and sought out a therapist. My first attempt was a total failure since the woman just did not understand important constructs like *complex* and Jung's anima, which I was just learning about. After two months, I decided to look elsewhere.

Following the advice of a friend who was also a Jungian analyst, I took a short introductory course on Jung at the New York Open Center in the spring of 2005. At the same time Karin and I had just read A. S. Byatt's prize winning novel *Possession*, where a famous Victorian male poet has a brief affair with a younger, unmarried woman. It brought the realization that, as Murray Stein (2006, 119) notes, "the anima is much more than only the gateway to sexuality for a man" and that something else was behind its powerful urgings. While I could never see myself succumbing to the ruinous impulse of infidelity, still the fires of my anima raged.

Jung proved relevant enough that in July I enrolled in a weeklong intensive, summer program at the New York Jung Foundation on "Power, Powerlessness, and Surrender." On the last day, the instructor discussed the synchronistically appropriate topic "Empowerment via Surrender." He was dynamic, a Jungian therapist in practice in Manhattan and seemed just the person who could address my anima issues. In my enthusiasm, I approached him about an introductory visit and arranged a time for a few weeks later. I subsequently did a Google search and discovered that he was active in the gay community and a champion cyclist. I wondered if he could relate to a nonathletic "straight" with anima problems. With this nagging uncertainty, I once again journeyed into the city on an extremely hot summer day, took the subway to the Upper East Side, and walked four blocks to his basement office. It really felt like a visit to Hades. After I recounted my story of infatuation with Karin, his advice to me was, "You need to get in touch with your inner masculine." I found this Delphic response baffling as I was, or thought I was, experiencing a problem with my inner feminine aspect, the anima.

Was this his issue (a countertransference compensation) or a valid assessment? It was hard to tell (although he turned out to be correct and turned out to be married). And how exactly does one reach the inner masculine?

My search continued as I read more of Jung during the fall. Then in January, 2006, I signed up for another course on Jungian Dreamwork taught by the president of the New York C. G. Jung Institute. That was all the encouragement my overactive anima needed as it immediately produced a major dream (described in chapter 5, Facing the Father Complex). In it, there appeared the symbol of the warrior-priest who could embrace the father rather than continue to fight him and then crossed over a bridge to a new phase of life. As the instructor said, "You're reclaiming your phallic, or masculine energy, from your father. And you're doing that by getting in touch with your feminine or compassionate, anima side."

This was the major breakthrough in resolving the block my father had bequeathed me in endlessly feeling victimized by and fighting with authority figures as in the struggle with the Dean of my retirement organization. So, it was the anima that first appears to seduce, but, if one has the strength to resist, really is a guide to the unconscious source of the turmoil—the father-complex, in my case. I felt the exhilaration of relief and release. I had achieved something that had even eluded Jung who, in his fight for sanity, steadfastly refused to acknowledge or heed the guidance of his anima as it appeared in his numerous dreams and voices (see Jung 1989, chapter VI). Instead, he dismissed them as "full of deep cunning" and ended this troubled period of midlife crisis by forcing his wife to accept a "permanent *ménage a trois*" with his mistress, Toni Wolff (McLynn 1996, 243).

As to Karin, clearly this was really not about her. It was my anima projection that she released, my father-complex, and finally my dreams. It is the Jungian shadow that one encounters upon entering the unconscious. I tried to bring her along with me since she shared the same major (father) complex that had led her into a series of dead-end affairs with men already committed to other women (the Freudian "repetition compulsion"), but she repeatedly maintained, despite her status as a therapist-in-training, "I'm not ready [for therapy]." I coaxed, cajoled, and threatened. I even suspended our conversation for a few months after a hostile and bitter outburst by her (animus) when I mentioned the need to capture her inner feminine in order to overthrow her father-complex. Otherwise she risked being forever trapped as an other-blaming victim. Her resistance was not that surprising.

James Hollis (2005, 65) has written that "[d]espite what we say to ourselves about wanting to know who we really are, there is a very strong chance that we will steer clear of decisive meetings with ourselves for as long as possible." These meetings didn't occur until my sixty-fifth year, so why should I expect Karin to be ready at twenty-nine. Nevertheless, it was clear that there was no longer the possibility for any further useful deep dialogue. It was not because I no longer cared for Karin; I did. It was not because, as the Buddhists say, "she was my teacher," reflecting back my anima issues, she was; but it was because it was the right time and the right thing to do. I had confronted both my anima and father complexes.

As Hollis (2005, 106–7) also noted, "All relationships begin in projection." Consequently, "the person who grew up with an impaired parent will be drawn to another troubled soul and reenact the familiar role of caretaker or enabler." I had encountered my impaired parents and had finally found meaning in my life (see chapter 10, The Return: My Transcendent Function). Like Odysseus, I had spent time with my Circe-anima and had visited Hades, and now it was time to return to Ithaka.

Once the fog of the anima had dissipated, it revealed a clearer reality and a decisive course of action. My wife's Penelope-like patience had been incredibly strained while I labored so long to understand what my anima was telling me. As Corbett and Rives (1991, 111) note, "When the anima acts as a forcible bridge to the unconscious, in the presence of negative complexes, this process is extremely painful." And so I bid Karin a heartfelt *auf weidersehen* to our e-mail correspondence knowing that such odysseys are terribly frightening, always lonely, but ultimately incredibly enlightening and transformative. Of course, Karin was initially upset, but she finally saw that it was not another rejection. I continually thanked her for playing a positive, rather than destructive, anima role that guided me to the fundamental, psychic source of my powerful anima eruption. Four years later, she sent me a note saying that she was about to enter psychoanalysis in preparation for a career as a depth psychologist.

Valentine's Day, February 14, 2008

The landscape of the body
is centered in the heart.

It's Valentine's Day, but it's also doctors' day for me. I have three appointments scheduled starting at 10:00 a.m.—first my eyes, then two for my bunion-deteriorated right foot. How romantic! Well, at least I'm prepared with a card, and even a gift for sweet Camille.

The first visit goes quite well. Dr. Fourman is on time, and happily my eyes are in very good shape. There are just the very first noticeable (to me) signs of cataracts. They're inevitable at my age, he says, but can be easily corrected. Then, at 11:40 a.m., it's next door (quite literally) to Dr. Apostolos Tasiopolis, who will examine the blood flow in my right foot. It's flowing quite nicely, he informs me, and I'm a good candidate for surgery. "Keep on walking," he says. "It's the best exercise at your age. And tell your wife it doesn't have to be aerobic!"

"Well," I say to the nurse, "the Greek gods and goddesses [my primary physician is Dr. E. Lila Augoustiniatos] are certainly smiling on me."

That afternoon, I visit Dr. Guido to see if there's any nerve damage in my foot. He is only prepared for a preliminary exam and schedules an electromyography test for February 29. That test also proved negative.

So, I've moved from head to toe, but, the heart is not to be neglected. On my way home from Dr. Tasiopolis's office, I stop and pick up a chilled bottle of Camille's favorite champagne, Gloria-Ferrer. When I arrive, I find a card at my place on the kitchen table. I add my own to her place, and then open the champagne to toast to "undying love."

I then read the short endearing message on my card while Camille waits to savor her champagne before opening hers. She knows it will contain a special, non-Hallmark insert—the latest stanza in an ongoing Valentine's Day poem I've been writing for the last ten years.

This year's installment has been inspired by a trip I've planned to Monument Valley and other national parks in the Southwest in mid-May.

Valentine's Day

To Camille, a valentine for all time

On this day my heart opens
    like an archetypal ancient canyon
Anticipating the overpowering vistas
    that crack open the meaning of our lives.

Scintillating red, of course, from
    the primordial sediment of the heart--
An amazing, awe-inspiring sight
    of the unity of nature's might;
A shadowy fear
    of the depth that is near.

On this day my heart opens
    to love and rejection;
To hope and dejection
    and, to you, of course.

Epilogue. I wrote this at 8:00 a.m. in the morning, and revised it slightly before presenting it to my Memoir Writing class a few hours later. The comments were minor, but, as always, very useful. One person said to me at lunch, "How's that a memoir; it just happened yesterday?"

"Well, it will be a memoir in six months," I replied. "And, I wanted to make sure that we all celebrated the spirit of Valentine's Day. After two preceding memoirs about death, I'm glad I did. We all need that Jungian balance in our lives." That is, we need balance not only between death and life, thinking and feeling, but also between the physical (ego) and the spirit (or Self).

That afternoon, just as I'd finished revising the memoir, the actual present I ordered for Camille arrived. It was a very highly recommended electric mattress pad. The card said, "Sweetheart, A warm heart deserves a warm body." She loved it and the mattress pad as well.

The Death of My Father Complex

You can have no dominion greater or less than that over yourself.

—Leonardo da Vinci (2008)

In the spring of 2010, I planned and celebrated my big 7-0 birthday on June 14 with a trip to Europe. First, my wife and I spent a week in the Loire Valley, staying in a small town called Amboise and, among other activities, visiting a number of famous local châteaux (or castles). We had booked a tour and initially found our only companions to be an elderly Japanese surgeon and his wife. In the morning, we visited Chenonceau—absolutely gorgeous and largely designed by women. King Henry II gave it to his mistress, Diane de Poitiers, who built a graceful, multi-arched bridge extending from the rear of the chalk-white chateau over the river Cher so that she could walk rather than row to the other embankment. After the king's death, her rival, the queen Catherine de Medici, took possession of the chateau and cleverly incorporated the bridge into the castle by enclosing it and adding a second-floor gallery above.

In the afternoon three other couples joined our tour—all Japanese. The French driver continued to provide short English descriptions of the châteaux but then played lengthy tapes in Japanese describing Cheverny, small, stately, classical, and finally the big behemoth at Chambord, with its distinctive, multitowered roof and Leonardo da Vinci designed, double-helix staircases. The surgeon leaned over to reassure me, saying, "The tapes are not nearly as informative as the tour guide's English descriptions. They didn't mention how the staircases allowed the king to come and go with his mistresses without the queen seeing them."

For you trivia fans, da Vinci spent his last few years in Amboise working for and tutoring the young French king Francis I, whose sprawling château towers above the town. Leonardo's residence, Clos Luce, is now a wonderful museum with an amazing (if you're there, as we were, in June) rose garden that was in full bloom with tens of thousands of brilliant red roses. The walls of the rooms and staircases contain framed quotes of Leonardo's "thoughts" (such as the one at the beginning of this section). It also reveals his dark, or shadow, side with displays of all his inventions used for combat, including plans for a machine gun that was actually built and used by the Russians centuries later. Perhaps that's why he said, "If a man overcomes a thousand men in battle, he wins a lesser victory than he who overcomes himself (da Vinci, 2008)." We left Amboise the day before my birthday and headed west along the Loire River road to Château de Chaumont (on the cover of the Michelin Guide to *Châteaux of the Loire*) and the place to which Catherine de Medici banished Diane de Poitiers. It is an archetypal château located on the top of a bluff overlooking the Loire with an amazing series of architect-designed gardens. After a wonderful lunch in a Michelin-recommended restaurant in the town just below the château, we drove through historic Blois, from which Joan of Arc lifted the siege of Orleans, and on to Chartres, with its classic Gothic cathedral to celebrate my birthday. The cathedral was open late that Sunday night featuring a free piano concert. It's both an awe-some and awe-inspiring place. You don't have to be Catholic to feel the spiritual forces streaming through the myriad, multi-colored, stained glass windows that lift you upwards.

On June 15, we drove to Orly Airport and flew to Oslo where Camille was to give two lectures at a local research hospital specializing in trauma care for stroke victims and those with spinal cord injuries. We arrived around midnight and entered a nearly deserted Gardermoen airport. There was only one store open, and everyone on the plane—and that included those with children—rushed into it. Curious, we followed along. It was the duty-free shop! It turned out that Norway heavily taxes wine and liquor, but that anyone entering the country can purchase two bottles tax-free. And everyone, including us, did!

I can't say enough about the hospitality and sensitivity of the Norwegian people. They outdo the Greeks, who, I thought, owned the concept of hospitality to strangers. We never would have found Vigeland Sculpture Park, for example, were it not for the seemingly magical intervention of one of those golden-haired goddesses who grace that country. The park contains the most remarkable outdoor art display I've ever seen with hundreds of life-size sculptures depicting the entire human condition and life cycle. Gustav Vigeland's bronze statues line both sides of a bridge that takes you to a huge fountain supported by other bronze figures, and finally to a circular set of steps each with triads of carved sand-stone figures culminating at the top in a monumental stele of writhing figures struggling to reach its summit. The park turned out to be the cultural highlight of my time in Oslo and is, as Michelin says, worth a trip there all by itself. And no, I didn't see the famous Munch *Scream* as there was a nationwide strike by security guards and all museums were closed as I discovered when I walked into the center of Oslo to the National Museum.

From Oslo, we flew to the western coastal town of Bergen where we purchased fish in the local outdoor market and made it into the centerpiece of an in-room dinner. We then took the famous "Norway in a Nutshell" trip that transports you by train and bus through incredible mountain scenery to a boat that meanders through part of a major fjord, dropping you at the world-famous Flam railway that ascends 850 meters and stops at (and almost in) a gigantic, rainbow-arched waterfall before it reaches the top at Myrdal. After Bergen we flew north of the

Arctic Circle to Svolvaer, the capital of the Lofoten Islands. It is a journey to another world. Jagged, snowcapped mountains and volcanic, mist-shrouded islands surround you. It's as if you've been transported back to the beginning of time. And, to add to the disorientation, the sun never sets at this time of year. We were just in time for the June 23 summer solstice celebration, when entire families gather around large bonfires and, as in America, cook, of all things, hotdogs. The only difference is that they were all wearing parkas, as the temperature was just a few degrees above freezing. We drove through some of the islands and also took a short cruise on the Hurtigruten—the major cruise company that runs luxury boats up and down the western coast. The vistas were amazing and the big boat actually managed to squeeze into a fjord on the way. Finally, four flights and twenty hours brought us back to JFK and the sweltering summer of Long Island.

Every journey, however, is simultaneously both an inner as well as an outer one. I'd hoped that Chartres cathedral with its soaring spaces and transcendent light would be the spiritual inspiration for such a major individuating revelation. While I was moved by the cathedral's immense exterior and interior beauty, there was no immediate epiphany. Instead, its impact was indirect providing the setting for the dramatic experience that was to unfold. It occurred during a makeshift dinner in an empty hotel breakfast room a stone's throw from Chartres cathedral. There, over some glasses of fine French champagne, my wife surprised me with a series of written testimonials from close friends and family.

Grace sent a cute card that, when opened, played the rousing theme song from the Indiana Jones movies and provided an appropriate fanfare for what followed. Mary wrote with characteristic humor, "Inside you are a wonderful, wise and thoughtful man of 'advanced' [wrong word], 'enough' [no not nearly] years." Rich observed, "Though you are much younger than my father would be were he still alive you remind me of him a little in that you slew some of your dragons where he ultimately didn't and that gives me a lot of hope for myself." In a similar vein, my Jungian muse, Elaine, said, "One of your great strengths is your willingness to face your own shadow and work with it, to move into the symbolic realm rather than acting out, which requires great self-restraint…And you have done this on your own" (see Foreword).

My emotions were rising as I got to the last testimonial from my son, Jer, who was entering his final year of medical school, and read his concluding words, "You have been the greatest Father that any son could ever ask for." Then, of course, there was no holding back the tears. Another miracle! I even heard in a spontaneous active imagination my father, Max, commenting in his usual demeaning way to me, "Ach, I should live so long." And now I answered, "*I* have." It was finally the end of my sense of inferiority instilled by Max—the negative father complex, as Jung would say. That lingering, perhaps ultimate, fear that my anti-Max parenting style (see chapter 4, Max) had been ineffective was at last lifted. I may have been, as my sons' Dreikurs' preschool course instructor said years earlier, "trying to be the too perfect parent," but now I was vindicated. Attaining the Biblical age of three score plus ten was, and still is, moving—and, most importantly—meaningful.

This, for me, was a trip of a lifetime and made turning seventy worth the wait. Camille was my true anima guide providing a perfect quarternity—two wonderful children, the wondrous trip, the miraculous testimonials, and most of all, her enduring love. As a Jungian, I can say Chartres definitely is a great place to find your-Self. Who knows? You may even slay a dragon there. I certainly did.

9 Health

My House Was Not My Home

Seldom or never does a marriage develop into an individual relationship smoothly and without crises; there is no birth of consciousness without pain.

—**C.G. Jung (1981, 192)**

In spring 1989, Camille and I accepted positions as professors in the psychology department at Stony Brook University. We had both become disillusioned with The University of Michigan. As Camille often said, success is overrated. Nevertheless, she viewed the Stony Brook job with some trepidation since she would have to redevelop its moribund Social Program into a new one called social/health psychology. And she viewed the move as somewhat of a payback to me since I'd never wanted to leave Northwestern for Michigan. However, when lightning actually struck twice on July 1, 1986 and both the academic units I was in ceased to exist via mergers into extremely hostile entities, it was clear that a move was essential.

While at Michigan, we had purchased ten acres of riverfront property and subsequently built a house. It had been a grueling two-year ordeal, and I was on record, published in the *Ann*

Arbor News, that I'd never do that again. That was before we started looking for a home in the Stony Brook, New York area. We loved contemporary, open houses such as the one we had built. The Three Village School District, where we wanted to live because our two boys were six and four years old, seemed to contain only old, musty, dark, and drab colonial homes. After looking at over fifty such homes, the Psychology Chair owned the one contemporary we saw, and he refused to sell as part of our recruitment package. He did, however, put us in touch with his builder.

Camille was ecstatic that we could build a new contemporary house in a cul-de-sac near the Setauket harbor and less than two miles from the university. And she kept noting, as my resistance crumbled, "It's a bargain at only $408,000." So, in our innocence of Long Island building, we flew to New York that July and signed a contract. The builder, who was also an architect, assured us that the home would be ready by February 1, 1990, when we arrived to start teaching at Stony Brook. That day, of course, came and the house was nowhere near habitable. We were, however, able to store most of our furniture and belongings in the garage and basement.

The months of the semester went by, and we were both overwhelmed with our university duties, getting our children settled in new schools, and dealing with the endless delays in construction. We did not know that our builder was an alcoholic or that he abused his subcontractors and then refused to pay them. All we knew was that little was getting done and what was completed did not seem to be of very high quality. We were learning about Long Island builders and what one really got for $408,000. Of course, that figure quickly escalated as we realized it included no lawn, since the builder had removed the topsoil and sold it, and not even any acceptable steps to reach the front door. The $408,000 soon became $500,000, and even then the quality was minimal or, as they say in the trade, "builder quality."

In May, with the school year ending, the builder started pressuring us to close on the house even though it was not completed and not yet in move-in condition. We resisted; the builder retaliated by confiscating our belongings. He even prevented my son from retrieving his tricycle from the garage. With all the stresses of her new job along with the new house, my wife was becoming increasingly agitated and depressed. The situation was exacerbated by her well-meaning, if insensitive, father who, as a professional electrician, constantly pointed out new, serious problems. The builder responded by having him barred from the premises. Finally, in early June, our attorney said we had to close. We returned to our new home, and my wife flung herself on the bed in fit of complete depression.

The depression did not lift, and Camille's friends and I became concerned. One of her former students, a professor in California, located a nearby therapist and persuaded Camille to see her. This seemed to work initially. But, as the year progressed, more and more problems with the house surfaced. We discovered a live 220-volt wire in the basement near where our children were playing, then that the entire electrical system was improperly installed with even the main fuse box upside down. We hired an attorney who discovered that the New York State Fire Underwriters had been bribed by our builder to obtain an inspection approval. He also discovered that our lawyer had also been bribed to force us to close.

With these revelations Camille's depression returned and worsened as the new school year began in the fall of 1991. Her therapist recommended antidepressants and sent her to a psychiatrist for evaluation. The psychiatrist agreed, but Camille's condition continued to deteriorate with sudden mood swings and erratic behavior. She seemed to be in torment, and I became alarmed. I called her therapist, but she was out of town.

The psychiatrist was also unavailable. In desperation, I tried the therapist who was seeing our son about problems adjusting to school and Long Island. She was an angel. She arranged for me to take Camille to see a psychiatrist in nearby Smithtown. All I had to do was persuade Camille that she needed to be hospitalized.

I don't know how I did it. It seems impossible to communicate rationally to someone who is no longer in a rational space. Somehow I coaxed Camille into the car for the trip. The diagnosis was quickly made—bipolar disorder or, more commonly, manic-depressive illness. Antidepressants, it turns out, will push people with bipolar disorder into full-blown mania, as happened to Camille. Fortunately, a simple treatment is available—lithium, which works in over 80 percent of such cases. And thankfully, it worked with Camille.

Epilogue. Camille has had only one recurrence of this problem again due to improper medications (see Black Day, White Knight). Her therapy uncovered the cause of her bipolar episode. When she was four years old, her insecure, Italian father decided he could only keep her seductively attractive mother from going out by pouring gasoline on her clothes in the closet and igniting them. Of course, the house burned down; the marriage ended; and so did Camille's happy childhood as she then lived with relatives until her mother remarried ten years later. Her desire to re-create that idyllic home—her house complex, as Jung would call it—left her vulnerable to housing-related problems.

Over the years, Camille's therapy successfully resolved her house complex. During that time, we painstakingly renovated the house to the point where we now really enjoy living in it. For me, the most important lesson was one Jung forgot to mention: just as you must become conscious of your own complexes in order to cope with them, it is equally important to do that for those you love. It has been the secret to the success of our marriage.

Black Day, White Knight

*And, when you want something, all the universe conspires
in helping you to achieve it.*

—Paulo Coehlo, The Alchemist

It was Saturday, September 29, 2007, and I was just sitting
down to lunch when the phone rang.

"This is Officer— from Sa…"

I thought I heard Sachem, a nearby school district, and
thought, "Oh no, did Andrew get another traffic ticket?"

The person corrected me, saying, "This is Officer McCoy
from the Sebastian, Florida, Police Department."

"Oh my God," I thought, "has something terrible happened
to Camille?" She was in Sebastian interviewing some clients
for a legal case. In fact, both Andrew and I had been extremely
concerned about her before she left and had asked her to post-
pone the trip. She had been so overwhelmed with work that
she was showing signs of extreme stress and exhaustion.

She refused, saying her therapist supported her decision
to go. All she had to do, he said, was "Take one step at a time."

Nevertheless, she seemed very confused and had difficulty
getting organized for the trip. I protested. "At least let me go
with you?" I implored.

But despite Andrew's forceful support for that idea, she
firmly rebuffed me, saying that I'd be bored. "Just help me get
all my things together," she said, adding for good measure, "Just
one step at a time. And I don't want you to miss your Memoir
Writing and Jung classes."

Then Officer McCoy continued. "Your wife has been
arrested and is in the Indian River County jail. She'll be arraigned
tomorrow."

"What!" I exclaimed. "I can't believe this. What happened?"

"Your wife tried to break into a truck just outside the Captain Hiram's Inn. When the woman driving the truck resisted and called for help, the hotel manager notified the police."

I was stunned. How could this be Camille? I wondered. But I had also been concerned about Camille. In fact, I'd been so alarmed after talking to her the night before when she called from Florida that I'd taken the liberty of sending an e-mail to her therapist, describing her agitated and disoriented condition. I had just sent if off when the phone rang.

"Is she all right?" I asked.

"I think she was having some sort of psychiatric event," he replied. "When I asked her where she lived, she said, 'In heaven.'" He had one question, "By the way, who's David?"

"Her therapist, but how can I contact her?" I inquired while resisting the urge to ask why he hadn't taken her to a hospital. Officer McCoy then gave me the number of the jail. When I called, I was informed that I was not allowed to talk to her; she would have to call me collect. That call never came as Camille's repeated requests to call me had been denied.

Later, I called the jail again and was connected to a male nurse who said that Camille had been sedated and was sleeping. "The earliest this will be resolved is 10:30 a.m. tomorrow when she'll appear before the judge," he told me. "She'll be here overnight."

In the meantime, I contacted Camille's therapist. Instead of calling the jail to offer any assistance, he put me in touch with his personal lawyer, whose only useful advice was to get down to Florida and be prepared to post bail.

I informed my sons, Jer and Andrew, about what had transpired. Jer urged me to get on the next plane to Orlando so I could be in court the next morning. Andrew found a 6:05 p.m., nonstop flight on Southwest from nearby Islip to Orlando and booked a round-trip ticket for me with a return ticket for Camille.

Andrew suggested that Camille's behavior might be due to the new sleep medications she'd been recently prescribed, particularly trazodone. Jer, our Web whiz and medical school student, immediately discovered that trazodone, a widely prescribed sleep drug, is an antidepressant. Moreover, if someone has bipolar disorder, it can cause major delusional and aggressive behavior.

I quickly packed, got directions from Orlando to the hotel, and had Andrew drive me to MacArthur Airport in Islip. I was on a quest to rescue my wife and everything seemed magically to fall into place. When we encountered a huge traffic jam on Nicolls Road on the way to the airport, Andrew didn't hesitate in cutting off to a side road, following the navigation system, and reentering a mile later ahead of the traffic. At the airport, I had time to arrange for an auto rental in Orlando. Luckily, a man determined to haggle for a lower charge occupied Hertz, and I rented from Avis, which, unlike Hertz, is conveniently located in the Orlando Airport.

The one hundred mile drive from Orlando to Sebastian also went smoothly as long as I successfully battled my anxiety over finding the proper exit on I-95. The only problem was locating the hotel when I arrived late at night in Sebastian; a phone call to the assistant manager solved that. He took me aside after I'd checked in and told me what he knew of that morning's event.

As I entered the room where Camille had been staying, I was confronted by chaos with papers, files and numerous Post-its that said "Trust David" scattered everywhere. And there on the nightstand was an open bottle of trazodone.

I awoke early the next morning, had breakfast, and decided not to wait until 10:30. Instead, I called the police department and was, once again, referred to the jail. I was told that I just had enough time to get to the courthouse for

Camille's arraignment. I followed their directions and entered what appeared to be a deserted courthouse in nearby Vero Beach at 8:30.

After passing through a metal detector, I was instructed by the guard to go up the stairs to Court Room 3. It was Kafkaesque. The courtroom was totally empty, except for a judge, a sergeant-at-arms, and one lone attorney. The current defendant being arraigned was on a television monitor. As I exited, the sergeant-at-arms followed and informed me that Camille had already been arraigned and that I could bail her out at the jail just a few miles away. She said the names of bail bondsmen would be posted on the wall there.

The jail was located just past Dodger Town, USA. As I was driving into the parking area, a car sped in front of me and a man jumped out. I hailed him, asking if this was the jail.

"Yes, this is it," he said moving rapidly toward the entrance.

"Do you know how I can find a bail bondsman?"

"I'm one. Wait a minute and follow me when I return."

Within seconds, he reemerged and we caravanned around the block to his office. I told him I needed to bail my wife out of jail. He entered the information into his computer and two mug shots of Camille appeared. "Bail has been set high at $10,000 since she's from out of state," he informed me.

"Well, what do you need and do you want cash?" I asked, worried that it was Sunday morning and all I had was $300 and Camille's business checkbook.

"In addition to my usual 10 percent fee, I'll need the full amount which will be refunded when the case is settled. You can make out two checks."

He filled out a form, gave me two receipts, and the names of some local lawyers he recommended. We then returned to the jail, where he told me it would probably take an hour for her release. I waited as the minutes dragged slowly away, wondering who would emerge.

Finally, Camille walked out dressed in blue prison pants with black-and-blue marks on her face and arms—a portent of her inner state. We embraced. She expressed her thanks for being rescued. I told her, "Sweetheart, in every fairy tale, the princess gets three successful rescues by her prince. This is your second."

Epilogue. Once Camille's physician verified to the court that her behavior was caused by trazodone and that it had been replaced by appropriate medications that stabilized her behavior, all charges were dropped. Camille told me that the trazodone induced a delusional state where she was in the final scene of the movie *Defending Your Life*, and, like Albert Brooks, she had to grab onto a moving vehicle in order to continue on toward heaven.

After two difficult weeks, Camille suddenly seemed her old self. It would be nice to conclude that we "lived happily ever after," but it took almost a year to work through the issues it raised. Those issues centered on Camille's desire to continue with her therapist.

I told Camille that she could continue meeting with her therapist to discuss how to handle the trauma work she was involved in, but I was adamant that she not continue any personal, in-depth work with him. He had misread her bipolar disorder by claiming, despite the medical evidence, that her symptoms were the result of childhood trauma and supported her going off lithium. Finally, he encouraged her to go to Florida when she was clearly dysfunctional because he misinterpreted the symptoms of her reaction to the new medication she'd started prior to the trip. I could never forgive myself if continued work with him led to a more serious catastrophe. I already felt traumatized by what had occurred. On the other hand, Camille said, "You're holding a gun to my head," and, referring to her house complex, "He's the one person who has discovered significant issues and who could actually heal me."

Nevertheless, I felt that I could not trust her therapist who knew just enough to be dangerous and that there was a significant risk of permanent harm—either psychological or physical—if she continued to see him. Camille's own research shows that spouses who lose a loved-one under these circumstances generally never recover from such guilt. However, she thought that she'd be permanently impaired without his continued therapy. Consequently, we were stuck.

This "tension of opposites" is not an unusual situation in heated arguments and conflicts according to Jungian analysts. For example, Marie-Louise von Franz (1995, pp. 68–69) notes that "one cannot go on living, because one tries to be too perfect in a one-sided way." That is, if one rigidly believes their position or solution is the only appropriate one, then any other position is intolerable and unacceptable. She adds that if we follow our moralistic Judeo-Christian ideals that we are right and must correct a wrong, "it would mean having to be killed and die as martyrs." Camille and I were each facing the mutual martyrdom of a psychological death. If I righteously prevented her for seeing her therapist, she said, "I don't know if I could ever forgive you." So, I'd be martyred. Similarly, if she saw him and had a relapse or worse, she would be martyred. What should we do? Von Franz says (p. 70), one must "suffer the conflict till something unexpected happens which puts the whole thing onto a different level." This soon occurred.

Camille had dinner with a friend who also had been David's patient. Her friend said, "Your husband is being very reasonable about this by letting you continue to do some work with David. Maybe you should get another opinion about the serious issues raised by him." This was just the kind of creative solution I was looking for.

I suggested that such an independent third party could either oversee David's work or preferably (for me) have David as a consultant if the person worked with Camille on these more central and difficult issues. Camille loved the idea and continued to see David for another year as I, along with her psychiatrist, acted as the "third party" monitoring her therapy with care and concern. Only after terminating with him was Camille able to get in touch with the feelings of betrayal that I and Andrew felt.

Synchronicity

A mystery so profound that none of us really seems to grasp it until it has indisputably grasped us, is that some force transcendent to ordinary consciousness is at work within us to bring about our ego's overthrow.

—James Hollis (2005, 70)

Some family mysteries are difficult to solve. Often they are buried in our genes and plague one generation after another. Andrew's most important mystery was the one that he and I had uncovered together and which made his twenty-first birthday dinner celebration a truly joyful moment.

Andrew had been a very difficult teenager. Of course, teens are all difficult by definition, but there was something else, something very serious, that was going on. His frustration with authority whether it be the high school guards over parking and room passes, teachers over late assignments or with us was disturbing. He would get into endless escalating confrontations and conflicts leading to time-outs and detention. He also seemed depressed and was often late getting to school or wouldn't go at all.

Camille and I, and the best medical minds in the area, couldn't figure it out. His psychologist thought it was simply adolescent oppositional-defiant behavior, but I was haunted by the thought of my younger brother, Ron. While my older brother and I had both gone to college and then obtained advanced degrees, Ron had never even finished high school. He has spent his life in low-level jobs just barely getting by. When Andrew would act out and draw us into those interminable, excruciating arguments, I would often conclude in total frustration and tears by blurting out, "I just don't want you to turn out like your uncle Ron [who had a high school GED and never attended college]." Little did I know how unconsciously, prophetic I was.

Well, after my nearly daily trips to bring him forgotten books and assignments, Andrew did manage to graduate from high school in 2003 and then enrolled in Drew University, a small, liberal arts school, located in Madison, New Jersey. Despite its initial impression as a nurturing environment, Andrew did not thrive there. The conflicts with the campus police over parking replaced those with the high school security guards. There were also problems with a number of his professors who responded in abusive, uncaring ways to his absences and missed assignments. For his part, Andrew always felt as if something inside was keeping him from achieving the academic perform-ance he desired.

Then a chance event set us on the path to revealing this secret. Andrew and I were visiting his physician who treats him for delayed sleep-phase syndrome when her assistant approached me. He thought Andrew's sleep problem might be related to another problem like ADHD, attention-deficit/hyperactivity disorder. He asked if I had read *Driven to Distrac-tion: Recognizing and Coping with Attention Deficit Disorder from Childhood through Adulthood* by Edward Hallowell and John Ratey. I did have a copy that my late mother-in-law had given me when her husband had been diagnosed with attention-deficit disorder (ADD). The book proved difficult to follow; just what you'd expect by an author (Hallowell) with ADD. It was repetitious and quite unspecific about the diagnosis.

A second event immediately occurred that Jung would label *synchronicity*, or a meaningful coincidence. I made a rare stop to check my mail in the Psychology Department from which I'd retired two years earlier. There I found Daniel Amen's book, *Healing ADD: The Breakthrough Program That Allows You to See and Heal the 6 Types of ADD.* I had lent the book to a colleague four years earlier, and now it suddenly was returned. Unlike *Driven to Distraction*, it was clear, concise, and contained diagnostic tests for various types of ADD. The written tests were to be taken by both the patient and a person who knows him or her. Andrew and I sat in our kitchen and were shocked to see that he scored quite high for Type 2: inattentive ADD, considered one of the harder variants to diagnose. A few months later, a physician at the New York University Child Study Center in Manhattan confirmed our preliminary diagnosis. It was suddenly clear that my younger brother, Ron, also has ADD as did, in all likelihood, my father before him.

Andrew and I hoped that this new information would give him a fresh start at Drew as the dean had promised when he, Camille, and I had met with her to discuss his recent diagnosis of ADD. Unfortunately, she once again turned down his petition for a withdrawal, or W, from a course where the instructor, an adjunct, had clearly taken advantage of his ADD by being nonspecific and late about the work requirements, by cajoling him to stay in the course after the withdrawal deadline with the promise that he could withdraw later, and then by reneging on that promise and awarding him an F even though he'd done most of the work. It became clear that the appeals process was a farce and that the dean would never overrule a faculty member even for a well-documented disability.

Andrew decided that was enough and transferred to Stony Brook University the following fall, 2005. He consistently received A's in all of his courses there, was sought out to be an undergraduate TA (teaching assistant), and worked in two research laboratories. He completed a major in psychology where he graduated with Honors and was class valedictorian. He is pursuing graduate work to become a therapist. And yes, Andrew is still forgetful and often late, but he is always striving to improve.

And so as my own distracted attention returned to dinner, I thought about how we could now share a glass of wine and offer a toast to successfully unraveling a family mystery. Camille added to Andrew, "Now that you're twenty-one, let's enjoy the present, look to a bright future, and affirm our love."

My Right Foot

Strive to preserve your health; and in this you will the better succeed in proportion as you keep clear of the physicians...

—Leonardo da Vinci (2008)

In July 2007, while walking extensively in San Francisco, my right foot began to hurt. The pain was constant as I walked and was quite uncomfortable. When I returned home in early July, I asked my primary care physician to recommend a foot specialist. The specialist was not available for over a month. Since my foot pain was chronic and I like to walk, I followed a friend's suggestion and saw a podiatrist who was not an MD. He explained that my big toe was no longer bearing the weight as I walked leaving the weaker second toe (or second metatarsal) to absorb the weight. This could be fixed with a new orthotic to replace the worn-out, ineffective ones that I had. Impressions were taken, and I was told they would be ready in a few weeks. That was July, but it wasn't until September that the orthotics actually arrived.

At that point, I thought I'd solved the problem with my right foot. It was not to be the case. After a few months, it was clear that the orthotics were not effective, and the pain was still present and persistent. I then decided to seek an appointment with the local physician originally recommended. I was surprised to learn that she specialized in foot surgery since I knew surgeons almost always recommend surgery. In early February, I met with the physician who was accompanied by a medical resident. She looked at my foot and gasped as she pointed out the various deformities. She catalogued them in an almost mocking way. I felt that my foot was the subject of a *Saturday Night Live* skit, and said so. Nevertheless, she convinced me to proceed with a number of tests to determine if surgery was warranted.

Over the next month, I had X-rays, a vascular test, two separate neurology exams, and an MRI to assess tarsal tunnel syndrome. When I met with the physician again, she informed me that I needed surgery, not just to remove the bunion on my big toe, but on every other toe as well. My head was spinning with her recommendations to fuse this bone, shorten that one, and put some screws in here and bolts there. It sounded like a prescription for Frankenfoot.

I decided I needed a second opinion, and to do that I needed copies of my medical records. I obtained a disk with a copy of the MRI. In order to obtain duplicates of my X-rays, I had to search out the Radiology File Room in the University Hospital. I also had to go to the nineteenth floor of the attached Health Sciences Center to purchase (at $0.75/page) a copy of my medical record. Luckily, I was able to have the results of both the neurological and vascular tests faxed to my home.

The next task was finding an expert for a second opinion. My wife, who's a whiz at searching the web, immediately located the Hospital for Special Surgery (HSS) Web site, which is http://www.hss.edu. There I found the head of the foot and ankle service. My wife then suggested I cross-check his name with those on *New York* magazine's list of "Best Doctors" that can be found at http://nymag.com/bestdoctors/. Sure enough, he was on the list. I immediately called and was, to my astonishment, able to get an appointment for the following week. In the meantime, I learned from my son who was in his first-year of medical school that HSS is the top-rated orthopedic hospital in the country. Many in my retirement group I discovered also used HSS. One colleague recommended that I contact a friend of his who had had extensive foot surgery. Amazingly, she had used the same physician at HSS that I'd found and said, "He is the only doctor who I would let touch my feet after having a negative experience out here."

So, during the Easter break, I traveled into The City for a consultation. While it lasted only 30 minutes and cost $450, it was well worth it. The doctor looked at my X-rays and, to my utter surprise, recommended that before considering surgery I first try a proper orthotic, as my new ones, it turned out, were not properly constructed. Even if I had surgery, he said it would only be necessary on the big toe and the neighboring second toe. Moreover, without even looking at my MRI, he assured me that I did not have tarsal tunnel syndrome. What he proposed was much less extensive, in every detail, than the local surgeon. The one—and only one—negative was that he did not accept Medicare. He then arranged for the certified orthotist to examine my foot and take impressions for new orthotics. A week later, they were ready and I have been walking pain free ever since.

Epilogue. I originally wrote this as a case study–cautionary tale for submission to my retirement group's (OLLI) monthly newsletter, *The Chronicles.* The following concluding paragraph and author information was added:

There are many lessons to be learned from this experience. First, always get a second opinion. Second, take advantage of the wealth of information that your OLLI colleagues are most willing to share. Third, use the web to find information about qualified professionals. There are some new sites like HealthGrades.com and Vitals.com that provide information for a fee on training, certification, disciplinary actions and patient ratings. Once all this is done, you will have to assess the effectiveness of the actual procedure recommended. This will be the subject of another article.

[Editor's Note: Paul Wortman is a retired Professor of Health Psychology where his research specialized on the assessment of innovative medical treatments.]

The editor, who was initially very enthusiastic, wanted to publish it in the next issue but was overruled by his editorial board. He sent me the comments of which the following was typical:

I strongly believe that an article of this type does not belong in *The Chronicles*. People will feel uncomfortable reading it. You cannot make *The Chronicles* into a medical bulletin. Before you know it, people will be writing about their illnesses.

I was not deterred by the criticism and subsequently submitted another article dealing with the controversy over the effectiveness of Vytorin in treating coronary-artery disease. The editor asked if I would submit similar columns in the future.

10 Spirituality

Alchemy

Think Jung on his birthday.

It was July 19, 2007, the fourth day of the New York Jung Foundation's program on "Soul Searching" and we were supposed to "gain knowledge of transcendence" through alchemy. The instructor wanted us all to pretend to be alchemists. Since no one really knows what that is—after all, alchemy was a mystery that even eluded Jung—I found myself passing on the plastic cup and the bottle of water she asked us to pour into it with our left hand. Maybe I was afraid of my high school chemistry experience where I blew up half the lab. And just the evening before there had been a huge explosion only a few blocks away. Surely that was a sign, maybe even an alchemical warning.

The woman next to me shook my hand when she realized I was not going to engage in this juvenile exercise in Let's Pretend. But, I wondered, how could I escape gracefully? Just then, the lecturer said, "Let's take a short break before we start." I quickly made my exit out the front door, passing my erstwhile neighbor who again congratulated me on my courage. Back at the hotel, Camille and I decided we'd salvage the day by having a nice lunch (it was Restaurant Week in New York) and then take the subway up to the Jewish Museum to see the Louise Nevelson exhibit.

Nevelson was the daughter of Jewish parents who'd fled the pogroms in the Ukraine at the turn of the nineteenth century and settled in Maine. Her father became a junk collector, mainly of wood. Nevelson, with their support, decided she wanted to be an artist and eventually ended up in New York City. Like her father, she collected discarded wood objects, but then transformed this *massa confusa*, or teeming disordered conglomeration, into an amazing, spiritually moving work of art. She did this by taking the *prima materia* of wood shards, typically pieces of bedposts, table legs, and other found objects; painting them black—the color, she said, that "contains all colors"; and, following her cubist approach, placed them in small, rectangular boxes. This truly was alchemy!

At age eighty, Jung (1970) had proposed in his last major work, *Mysterium Coniunctionis*, that alchemy was really a psychological process where matter is broken apart (a process called *separatio*) and then united with spirit—the conscious with the unconscious—to produce a new, higher unity (or *coniunctio*) that was the goal of personal development that he called *individuation*. And here it was in the works of Nevelson where the primal, feminine material—wood—was covered in the feminine color—black, and literally transformed.

Nevelson's own life remarkably followed this alchemical process as Jung might have predicted. She had to separate from her parents in Maine, and then later, as a young mother with a son, from her husband in order to pursue her career as a woman and an artist. In her fifties, she found the artistic wholeness within herself as expressed in a room-sized work depicting the unity of marriage. Two large figures represent the bride and groom, complete with witnesses and a religious setting that fill a rectangular space. And, unlike all her other works, everything is painted white. It is truly the *hierosgamos,* or sacred wedding, that joined the opposites—the feminine and the (masculine) artist, matter and spirit—a transformation of both Nevelson and her work. At that point, she was able to extend her art out into the world in a compassionate way. This is exemplified in the very next piece in the exhibition—a wall-sized, cubist, black wooden monument to the victims of the Holocaust.

At that moment, I thought I'd had a true alchemical experience. But the day was not over, and the climax, my *coniunctio,* was yet to come. That evening Camille and I went to one of our favorite restaurants. We were given a special table, separated from all the others, that looked out the front window. As we finished our meal, a young couple appeared and waved. I waved back. They opened the door, and I told them to come in, that the food was great. They entered and came over to me—the husband and his wife, who was carrying their infant son. The boy looked intensely at me, and suddenly he seemed transformed. His eyes opened wide, a numinous smile burst across his face, and then both his arms flung wide open to embrace me as he reached his hand out with his forefinger extended to touch me. It was a sacred moment of unity—the father, the mother, the son, and I, like Abraham, a spiritual father. Camille watched all this in amazement, and said later, "If I hadn't been there and you'd told me this, I would have said, 'You're crazy.'"

A week later, on July 26, 2008, I wrote this memoir on what would have been Jung's 133rd birthday.

Project Apollo

The decisive question for man is: Is he related to something infinite or not? That is the telling question of his life.

—C. G. Jung (1989, 325)

In May 1962, President John F. Kennedy spoke at our college graduation. While he joked that he now had the best of all possible worlds—"a Harvard education and a Yale [honorary] degree," he's now best remembered for the short-lived dream of Camelot; the Cuban missile crisis; and two lasting, political accomplishments—the Peace Corps and developing the space program by sending men to the moon within the decade. The latter became known as Project Apollo. I guess this name was chosen because the Greek sun god, Apollo, sounded more positive than did the moon or Luna. One can only imagine all the "lunacy" jokes if that more accurate name had been chosen. As fate, or the gods, would have it, within a year, I would be working on Project Apollo commissioned by President Kennedy.

By that time, I had just completed my first year of graduate school in computer science at Carnegie Mellon University (CMU). My advisor, Allen Newell, had lined up a summer job for me at MIT's Lincoln Labs located on the Hanscom Field Air Force Base in Lexington, Massachusetts. MIT had the contract to write the computer code for the Apollo mission and I, and another CMU grad student, was hired as part of the small group of programmers to work on it. The job appealed to me because I liked programming, and it was only two hours from my parents' home in Connecticut.

MIT, along with CMU, was emerging as a leading academic research center in the new field of computer science. Since the computer work required a secure, off-campus military site,

MIT was using a remote programming system they had developed called Project MAC, for Machine-Aided Cognition. One sat at a terminal and typed, rather than keypunched, computer code. In this case, it was in Fortran. The programs were then immediately assembled, that is translated into machine language, and run at MIT's computer center twelve miles away in Cambridge. Within minutes, the output or results were printed. It was addicting, just like a human Skinner box where we were the pigeons pecking on the keyboard and our reward pellets were the outputs of our programming efforts. As we fell into this 24/7 reinforcement routine, we renamed MAC to stand for "Man and Concubine."

Our small group was treated to the latest videos from the space program. We were the first, outside of NASA, to see the astronauts walking in space and performing all the other technological feats that eventually took man to the moon. I only worked two summers at Lincoln Labs and never knew exactly what our programs were being used for. I guess in those youthful, naïve days, I was too focused on graduate work and dating to think much about a few summers' work outside of Boston. However, Joseph Campbell (1972) captured the Jungian significance of the Apollo mission when he said, "That moon flight as an outward journey was outward into ourselves….I mean… that trip has transformed, deepened, and extended human consciousness to a degree and in a manner that amount to the opening of a new spiritual era" (p. 239).

Just as the mighty Saturn rocket carried men through the arc of space, it also took me through a longer arc of time. In spring 2006, I decided to respond to two Yale classmates, Steve Buck and Chris Bent, who were debating the Iraq war. I wrote a Jungian analysis that was posted on our class (Yale, 1962) web site (www.yale62.org), "George W. Bush's Democratism: A Jungian Response to Buck and Bent." I immediately received an e-mail from Chris, who supported the war. His e-mail name was Frogfather, and he'd been a Navy Seal during the sixties. Now he was a retired, Christian conservative living in Florida and very active in his church. As our e-mail conversation progressed, I learned we shared a common history beyond college. His proudest moment as a Seal was being the first man to open the bobbing capsule and welcome the Apollo astronauts home upon their return from space.

Suddenly, it hit me that we, two, were both joined in this event. Despite our seeming differences—he, a Southern, red-state conservative, and I, a Northern, blue-state liberal; he, for the Iraq war, and I, against; he, a devout Christian calling *The Da Vinci Code* "a blasphemy"; I, a cultural Jew who thought, like Jung, that Dan Brown's book heralded the needed resurgence in the "sacred feminine" to restore the patriarchal imbalance pervading the world—that we could work together on arguably the most important technological and consciousness-expanding adventure of our generation. For all I knew, my computer programs may well have been guiding the Apollo rocket through liftoff to landing. And there waiting for them was another classmate, Chris. I thought if only we could find that unity of purpose again.

I concluded our e-mail conversation by sending Chris the following poem, "We Are One," which is my credo. He responded by saying, "Hey, your poem is absolutely marvelous…that is how I choose to remember you…"

We Are One

The compass spins madly
eternally seeking the
one true direction.
Museums overflow
weary with fragments
scattered by legions of men
who hacked their way
through history
claiming to follow the
one true path.
Verily, when we see clearly
that all drink from a spring
of the one pulsing artery,
then shall it be said,
we are one.

We carry with us
the ancient banners
of the gods that sheltered us.
From Artemis to Zoroaster
they encompass the
alphabet of soul
that spells the
one true word.
Hallelujah! It is revealed:
We are the Alpha and Omega.
Before the last trumpet of time
will all sin be cast aside
by compassion?
Will all revenge be annulled
by love?
Will all salvation be sealed
by peace?
For surely we will only bathe

in that pure river when
we are One.

From afar dancing
on golden rays
twirls the one blue ball
where we cling to the
one true dream
of all men and gods.
From Thebes to Rome,
from Lhasa to Kyoto.
from Jerusalem to Wittenberg,
from Babylon to Mecca,
let the word go forth.
Hear O nations of the world,
We are the Lords your Gods;
We are One.

We gather now
sons and daughters
as the world's
one true congregation
to face the fear
of our differences.
O my brothers and sisters,
when we have banished blame,
conquered craving, and put aside pity,
then will darkness become light as
emptiness becomes non-emptiness
and suffering surrenders to
the noble truth of nirvana's path.

Here, and only here,
annealed in the
scars of our ancestors,
we can live together when
We are truly One.

The Return: My Transcendent Function

The shuttling to and fro of arguments and affects repre-
sents the transcendent function of opposites. The confron-
tation of the two positions generates a tension charged
with energy and creates a living, third thing—...that leads
to a new level of being, a new situation.

—C. G. Jung (1969e, 90)

After resigning from the committee positions in my retirement community in early February, 2006, as a compensa-
tory resolution derived from a major dream (see chapter 5,
Facing the Father-Complex), I wondered what further material
would emerge. This was soon provided by the following message from my unconscious:

Nobel Prize dream

I'm in a room with Camille and told there's a phone call. I assume
it's for Camille since she's the phone person in our family. However,
it's for me. It's from an old colleague whom I haven't seen for almost
twenty years. Suddenly I'm walking on the street with the phone, and
he asks me, "Have you heard about the Nobel prizes?"

I reply, "I think someone told me they're in the process of making
the [Nobel Prize] awards."

He continues, "Well, I have good news for you."

I'm taken aback and ask, "Are you on the [awards] committee?"

He says, "Well, I can't really answer that, but be prepared."

"Prepared for what?" I inquire. I'm totally in disbelief since I've
been retired for five years and my research was not very visible,
especially at that level. He continues to talk positively about this,

but my cell phone doesn't seem to be working very well. All I hear is "blueberry…lock." At that point, I am overwhelmed with a joyful kind of relief or release. I cannot even continue walking. Instead, I have to lie down on the sidewalk quivering and crying.

Then I woke up.

There was a very clear complementary message here that my dream course instructor and I both perceived. The "joyful" release that I'd been seeking was achieved by ending the repetition in fighting father figures such as the dean and by achieving meaningful, "Nobel" or noble work. I realized that I'd been trapped in a series of such battles that had frozen my growth (or, as Jung would call it, individuation) and it was time to recognize the negative father-complex, cross over the bridge, and rise above it (as in my initial dream). But was that all?

Was there a symbol hidden in the dream uniting the oppositional forces in the conscious and unconscious? Jung calls this process and the unifying symbol that results "the transcendent function" and warns that "dreams are unsuitable or difficult to make use of in developing [it], because they make too great demands on the subject (Jung, 1969e, 77)." Of course, I missed that symbol as did my instructor. It wasn't until two years later (in early 2008) that the mystery was solved.

One early spring night, I had a dream of which I remembered only the beginning and the end. Strangely, it involved a large blueberry that appeared at both times. First, it was sliced, and at the conclusion, it was whole. By itself, it would appear meaningless, but in the context of the above dream and a conscious event that occurred about the same time, it took on significant meaning. Blueberry was the symbol resulting from the clash of the conscious and unconscious. It was my transcendent function.

**Earth from Space: "The Blue Marble"
Courtesy NASA Goddard Space Flight Center
and the Visible Earth Team**

The earth-shaped and earthlike blueberry is my favorite fruit and is my favorite color. It is one of the magical fruits of the earth associated with improved mental functioning. So it combines the chthonic aspects of the nurturing feminine with the thinking masculine.

At the time of that dream I had engaged in a dialogue with a former college classmate who, in true Jungian fashion, stood opposed to me politically, geographically and even religiously (see preceding Project Apollo). Nevertheless, we had unknowingly come together in working on the space program that sent the first man to the moon. Moreover, the seminal image in the poem I shared with him, "We Are One," was of the "one blue ball"—the earth seen from space, which is arguably the archetypal image of that era and is the spiritual manifestation of the blueberry. All of this was crystallized by the second dream. My transcendent function was a true *unus mundus*, or one world that united the oppositional forces in my conscious and unconscious.

On further reflection, it became apparent that there was also a mythic aspect (from the collective unconscious) that reversed the Biblical story of The Fall from God's grace of Adam and Eve. The former colleague had, in real life, betrayed me just like the serpent in the garden. He had been a father-mentor who tried to wrest control of a major research project I had developed (see chapter 3, My Work: The Consensus Development Program Evaluation). Now the unbidden fruit, the blueberry, emerged from the unconscious where Adam and Eve had originally resided and restored, for me, that lost balance. It was the true joining of matter and spirit—a joyful return.

In the Valley of the Gods:
A Prayer on the Path

*Where I am, I don't know, I'll never know, in the silence
you don't know, you must go on, I can't go on, I'll go on.*
—Samuel Beckett, The Unnamable (1959, 418)

Amidst the brutal beauty of The Valley of the Gods
you travel on the path of the ancient ones.
It is a pilgrimage paying homage
to massive, crimson stone monoliths.
Do not bow down; do not worship them as idols.
They are your guardians—spiritual markers
of an ineffable force that speaks an eternal language
as they lift you upward in an azure embrace.

Amidst the brutal beauty of the unscrolled desert
you walk between dawn and dusk; awe and anxiety;
love and loss; faith and fear; spirit and serpent.
A power of timeless unity caresses your being.
This is the place where you are lost;
where you must wander; where you must call out
for redemption, renewal, resurrection.

Amidst the brutal beauty of the empty wilderness
you will find the hidden trail. It is the path
to Mt. Sinai; it is the path to the Mount of Olives;
it is the path to Mecca. It is the path of paths
that all must take. It beckons to you.
For only here amidst the brutal beauty
can you at last find your self.

Amen.

The Valley of the Gods, Utah

Afterword: Who Am I?

All that is gold does not glitter; not all those that wander are lost.

—J. R. R. Tolkien, The Fellowship of the Ring

What a seemingly simple question to ask. Of course, my name is Paul Wortman, the second son of Julia and Max Wortman...STOP! Did I get even these basic facts correct? And is it important?

This is not a question a sixty-something, Ivy League-educated, retired psychology professor should even be contemplating. The meaning of life, or the meaning of my life—now there's a BIG question to consider. But, if one's basic assumptions are wrong, can one begin to pursue these issues? That's my dilemma.

You see, in 1974, my recently divorced mother was visiting Camille and me in our home just outside Chicago. As we drove into that city, my mother was in a mood to reflect and to reveal. Now the last thing children ever want to hear about is the sex life of their parents. Nevertheless, my mother felt compelled to share a salient detail. She related how she had really tried to be a good sex partner for my father and had decided, as an experiment, that she would make herself available whenever he asked. Well, night after night, he would ask, and she would comply. This went on for over a month until she was worn out by his sexual insatiability. She then had to resort to the old ruse saying, "Not tonight, dear; I have a headache." And then to emphasize the point about my father's sexual failings, she added the coup de grâce, "And he only knew one position—the missionary position!"

It was just beginning to occur to me that she must have known some other positions—but how?—when she unloaded the really big sexual bombshell. She said she'd had a brief affair with a very distant cousin, named Sellwitz, who owned a carpet store in southern Connecticut. It began just before I was born in the back room of his store. In a flash two anomalous events from my college years jumped to mind in a completely new perspective. Oh my God! Did that explain it?

The "it" involved the decision that led to my enrolling in Yale and a subsequent encounter that took place in New Haven. One of the shining, positive memories of my mother was how, without even asking me, she realized I was no longer interested in becoming an engineer and acted to support me in choosing a college. With the exception of Yale, which had a separate school of engineering, I had only been admitted to engineering schools. In fact, I had received a full scholarship to Rensselaer Polytechnic Institute (RPI) in Troy, New York, and had sent in my acceptance. My mother called Yale and intercepted my letter of declination, and then called RPI. She not only told them I was not coming but also proposed they award the scholarship to my best friend, Gerry Leverant. And they did! Needless to say, once at Yale, I never stepped into their Sheffield School of Engineering.

A second event occurred while I was a student at Yale. My mother arranged for me to have holiday dinner with a distant relative who lived not far from campus. His last name was Sellwitz. Once I arrived, I remember being stunned. The man looked just like me—dark brown hair, brown eyes, same long oval face with a big nose, and even the same horned-rimmed glasses. It was so eerie that it stuck in my mind all those years.

So, as I drove on with my mother and Camille, my eureka experience continued to unfold. Could I be the product of that illicit union? Both my brothers were blond with hazel-blue eyes—just like my father, but not me. My father was OK with them, but not with me. Both were born in October; I, in June. My father treated both my mother and me with contempt, saying many despicable things with the potential for, and sometimes with, actual physical violence, but never threatened either of my brothers. Was this liaison the cause? All of this flashed through my mind.

For some reason, I did not want to know and did not follow up on my mother's revelations with questions of my own. There was just too much trauma to deal with, and I wasn't ready to handle it. After a false start at Duke University, I was trying to reestablish my academic career at Northwestern, and that took all my energy. And so, here I am faced with that primal enigma, who am I? My answer is simple: it's not where you start from, but where you end up. My Jungian journey to individuation has led to many insights that have produced both inner and outer growth, including a deep, compassionate spirituality. These memoirs have told that story in both prose and poetry. In that spirit, I conclude with a poem dedicated to Jung.

Jung's Dharma

Circle round O my analysands
as night descends like a primordial blanket.
Observe, at the center, the flames
of the fire, the fire, the fire, the fire.

The fire that warms
is the fire that burns.

Its Promethean glow lets you see
the other more clearly than the self.
Contemplate the flickering silver spears
of the light, the light, the light, the light.

The light that illuminates the eyes
is the light that casts the shadow.

Draw the shades of the day
and let its last seed-like ember
burst forth in a dazzling dream
of the unity, the unity, the unity, the unity.

The unity of joy and pain, seeing and knowing
is the unity of two into one.

References

Amen, Daniel. G. 2001. *Healing ADD: The Breakthrough Program that Allows You to See and Heal the 6 Types of ADD*. New York: G. P. Putnam's Sons.

Beckett, Samuel. 1959. *Molloy Malone Dies and the Unnamable Three Novels*. New York: Grove Press.

Bond, D. Stephenson. 2003. *The archetype of renewal: Psychological reflections on the aging, death, and rebirth of the king*. Toronto, Ontario, Canada: Inner City Books.

Campbell, Donald T. 1991. Methods for the experimenting society. *Evaluation Practice* 12: 223-260.

Campbell, Joseph. 1972. *Myths to live by*. New York: Penguin.

Coehlo, Paulo. 2006. *The Alchemist*, 2nd ed. New York: Harper Collins.

Corbett, Lionel, and Cathy Rives. 1993. *"The Fisherman and His Wife"* The anima in the narcissistic character. In *Psyche's stories*, vol. one. eds. Murray Stein and Lionel Corbett. Wilmette, IL: Chiron Publications.

Da Vinci, Leonardo. 2008. *The thoughts of Leonardo da Vinci*. Amboise, France: Editions du Clos Luce.

Frank, Jerome. 1968. *Sanity & survival: Psychological aspects of war and peace*. New York: Random House.

Hallowell, Edward M, and John J. Ratey. 1995. *Driven to distraction: Recognizing and coping with attention deficit disorder from childhood through adulthood.* New York: Touchstone.

Hillman, James. 1977. *Re-visioning psychology.* New York: Harper Collins.

Hollis, James. 2005. *Finding meaning in the second half of life.* New York: Gotham Books.

Johnson, Robert A. 1993. *Owning your own shadow.* San Francisco: Harper.

Joyce, James. 1990. *Ulysses.* New York: Vintage.

Jung, Carl Gustav. 1968. Psychological aspects of the mother archetype. In *Collected works,* vol. 9, part I, second ed. Princeton, NJ: Princeton University Press.

Jung, Carl Gustav. 1969a. Instinct and the unconscious. In *Collected works,* vol. 8, second ed. Princeton, NJ: Princeton University Press.

Jung, Carl Gustav. 1969b. The soul and death. In *Collected works,* vol. 8, second ed. Princeton, NJ: Princeton University Press.

Jung, Carl Gustav. 1969c. The stages of life. In *Collected works,* vol. 8, second ed. Princeton, NJ: Princeton University Press.

Jung, Carl Gustav. 1969d. Synchronicity: An acausal connecting principle. In *Collected works,* vol. 8, second ed. Princeton, NJ: Princeton University Press.

Jung, Carl Gustav. 1969e. The transcendent function. In *Collected works,* vol. 8, second ed. Princeton, NJ: Princeton University Press.

Jung, Carl Gustav. 1970. *Mysterium coniunctionis. Collected works,* vol. 14, second ed. Princeton, NJ: Princeton University Press.

Jung, Carl Gustav. 1981. Marriage as a psychological relationship. In *Collected works,* vol. 17, fifth ed. Princeton, NJ: Princeton University Press.

Jung, Carl Gustav. 1985. The significance of the father in the destiny of the individual. In *The father: Contemporary Jungian perspectives,* ed. A. Samuels, 229–247. New York: New York University Press.

Jung, Carl Gustav. 1989. *Memories, dreams, reflections* (A. Jaffe, ed.). New York: Vintage Books.

Jung, Carl Gustav. 1991. Psychological Types. *Collected works,* vol. 6, paperback ed. London: Routledge.

Jung, Carl Gustav. 2006. *The undiscovered self.* New York: Signet.

Lindorff, David. 2004. *Pauli and Jung: The meeting of two great minds.* Wheaton, IL: Quest Books.

McLynn, Frank. 1996. *Carl Gustav Jung.* New York: St. Martin's Press, 1996.

Myers, Isabel Briggs with Peter B. Myers. 1980. *Gifts differing: Understanding personality type.* Palo Alto, CA: Davies-Black Publishing.

Neihardt, John G. 2000. *Black elk speaks.* Lincoln: University of Nebraska Press.

Pascal, Eugene. 1992. *Jung to live by.* New York: Warner Books.

Shirer, William L. 1960. *The rise and fall of the Third Reich: A history of Nazi Germany.* New York: Simon and Schuster.

Simple justice. 1993. PBS documentary, The American Experience series. Boston: WGBH.

Stein, Murray. 2006. *The Principle of Individuation.* Wilmette, IL: Chiron Publications.

Tick, Edward. 2001. *The practice of dream healing.* Wheaton, IL: Quest Books.

Tonkiss, Maria J. P. 2006 *¡Adelante! Achieving "The American Dream."* Pittsburgh, PA: Dorrance Publishing Co.

von Franz, Marie-Louise. 1995. *Shadow and evil in fairy tales.* Boston: Shambala Publications.

Wortman, Paul M. 2004. The paper bag. *Journal of Medical Humanities* 25:224–25.

Wortman, Paul M., and Fred B. Bryant. 1985. School desegregation and black achievement: An integrative review. *Sociological Methods & Research* 13: 289–324.

Wortman, Paul M., Amiram Vinokur, and Lee Sechrest. 1988. Do consensus conferences work? A process evaluation of the NIH Consensus Development Program. *Journal of Health Politics, Policy and Law* 23:469–98.

Yeats, William Butler. 1996. *The collected poems of W. B. Yeats* (rev. second edition), ed. Richard J. Finneran. New York: Scribner.

About the Author

Although I'm a Professor Emeritus of Psychology who has been teaching courses on Carl Gustav Jung only since I retired, I did not do what most of you probably think of as psychology, that is, psychotherapy. Nevertheless, I have encountered firsthand my share of psychological problems—attention-deficit disorder, anxiety disorder, bipolar disorder, depression, panic attacks, and post-traumatic stress disorder. Each encounter scraped away more of my insensitivity and ignorance and, in a true Socratic sense with Jung's invaluable assistance, led to significant healing and insight.

The major events that cover the chronology of my life are recounted in my memoirs and need not be reiterated here. What is most important to know is that at the bottom of all this suffering I have found that Jungian Self with its deep well of compassion. The following poem, with apologies to Whitman's "Out of the Cradle Endlessly Rocking," tries to capture this feeling that seemed even to elude Jung at the end of his autobiography, *Memories, Dreams, Reflections*.

The Word to Cherish

Why shouldn't I blurt it out?
You've heard it many times, but never enough.
You know it, but must relearn it at every age—
    as a child, as a spouse, as a parent.
It's just a plain, unadorned word
    that sets the ethereal dust to twinkling.

Some say it's death, death, death, death,
    but now I know better.
Death's for children of rapier-tongued parents
    whose scabrous wounds have bound the word
    in anger and sadness.
Death haunts the bitter residues of life,
but flees to insignificance when
this word plucks an inner chord.

Some say it's hope, hope, hope, hope.
But, it is what is hoped for.
Yes, I know too well, you may not have gotten it.
But, you can always give it.
Hope, after all, is just a pawnshop ticket
    waiting to redeem it.

So now I say it's love, love, love, love.
Love that kisses the emerging brow of the
    newborn sun;
love that howls in the night as the merging of
    earth and sky.
love that hugs Demeter's spring rain tightly
    to Persephone's sprouting crop;
love that launches the spirit into the universe's
    eternal sparkling embrace.

Yes, I say all this and more.
The clapping of the sea's waves,
the whispering of the woodland's wind,
the twittering of the sky's birds
all sing that one truest word.
What say you?

Paul M. Wortman
East Setauket, NY
January 1, 2011

9849544R0015

Made in the USA
Charleston, SC
18 October 2011